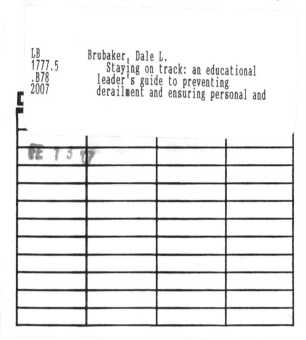

For Allison and Leigh Ann

Second Edition

STAYING on TRACK

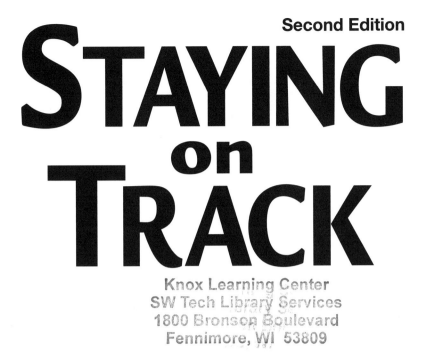

An Educational Leader's Guide to Preventing Derailment and Ensuring Personal and Organizational Success

Dale L. Brubaker   Larry D. Coble

CORWIN PRESS
A SAGE Publications Company
Thousand Oaks, California

For information:

Corwin Press
A SAGE Publications Company
2455 Teller Road
Thousand Oaks, California 91320
www.corwinpress.com

SAGE Publications Ltd
1 Oliver's Yard
55 City Road
London EC1Y 1SP
United Kingdom

SAGE Publications India Pvt. Ltd.
B-42, Panchsheel Enclave
Post Box 4109
New Delhi 110 017 India

Printed in the United States of America

Library of Congress Cataloging-in-Publication Data

Brubaker, Dale L.
Staying on track : an educational leader's guide to preventing derailment
and ensuring personal and organizational success / Dale L. Brubaker, Larry D.
Coble.— 2nd ed.
    p. cm.
Includes bibliographical references and index.
ISBN 1-4129-3935-6 (cloth) — ISBN 1-4129-3936-4 (pbk.)
    1. School management and organization—Vocational guidance—United States.
2. School administrators—Employment—United States. 3. Career
development—United States. 4. Educational leadership—United States.
I. Coble, Larry D. II. Title.
LB1777.5.B78 2007
371.2′01—dc22

                                                2006002895

This book is printed on acid-free paper.

06   07   08   09   10   10   9   8   7   6   5   4   3   2   1

Acquisitions Editor:	Kylee Liegl
Editorial Assistant:	Nadia Kashper
Production Editor:	Kristen Gibson
Typesetter:	C&M Digitals (P) Ltd.
Cover Designer:	Scott Van Atta

Contents

Preface

Expectations: School board members, parents, teachers, and others look forward to a new beginning as a superintendent comes on board. A superintendent, parents, school board members, teachers, and students have high hopes when an assistant principal or principal begins his or her tenure in a school. Newly appointed educators anticipate a bright future as they sense the excitement in the air after their arrival. The expression honeymoon period captures the optimism of this marriage between those already in the educational setting and the newly appointed leader. And who wants to talk about possible problems during a honeymoon?

It is, however, a reality of today's society that individuals and organizations ignore widespread sociological and psychological trends—and do so at considerable risk to themselves and others. References to reforming, restructuring, and rethinking tell us that we are grasping for words to describe ferment and a more hopeful future in our schools and school systems. There is one political force that has greatly increased in emphasis since the first edition of *Staying on Track: An Educational Leader's Guide to Preventing Derailment and Ensuring Personal and Organizational Success* (1997), and this political force has created profound changes in the culture of schools and schooling: legislation mandating accountability in general and high-stakes testing in particular. Federal pressure in the form of the No Child Left Behind (NCLB) Act triggered state, district, and school actions that significantly influenced the lives of administrators, teachers, students, and their parents. For many politicians and educational leaders, *measurement* was no longer considered *one kind* of assessment: It instead replaced the word *assessment*.

Readers of the first edition of our book therefore urged us to revise *Staying on Track* with the new political realities in mind. We thus begin the second edition with a new chapter, titled "Accountability and High-Stakes Testing." It is our view that this political force influences all other factors facing educational leaders.

In the midst of this age of challenge and hope, a term has become part of our vocabulary as educational leaders—*derailment* (see Brubaker & Coble, 1995). This term is useful in two ways: (1) to keep you, the individual, on track with your career path goals and (2) to help others in your organization, for whom you as an educational leader are responsible, to stay on track, thus minimizing the waste of organizational resources. We would do well to remind ourselves that there is always interaction between the individual and the organization. It is this *transactional context* of interactive forces that helps us see that both individuals and organizations can derail. In short, derailment has both a personal and an organizational face (Lombardo & Eichinger, 1995), and by *organizational face*, we mean the face of the school or school system.

Our thesis throughout this book is that creative leaders use their talents to help others identify and use their talents within organizational structures (Brubaker, 2004). When this definition of creative leadership is realized, derailment can be prevented or dealt with in a constructive way to the advantage of both the person and the organization—the school and the school system.

It is obvious in talking to educational leaders in our school systems that there is a career path ladder with an accompanying reward system. The educational leader begins his or her trek with a dream: "I wonder what it would be like to be a school administrator." With the dream in mind, the potential leader enters into a preservice program, usually at a university, to acquire certification. Once certification is earned, the candidate uses his or her network of friends and acquaintances to get inside information as to how to apply for and get a position as an assistant principal. After serving as an assistant principal, most educational leaders apply for a principalship. Some then move on to a central office position, in some cases an assistant superintendency. A few of these leaders apply for and are named superintendents of schools.

Our definition of educational leader derailment is concise and precise: An educator *wants* what he or she considers a better position but is not assigned the position by the powers that be. Or an educator *wants* to retain his or her present position and is demoted or dismissed. It should be clear from our definition that the educational leader's expectations are central to the concept of derailment. We make this point because of what has repeatedly happened during leadership seminars when we introduce the concept of derailment. One or more participants provoke a good deal of discussion, indeed debate, by making comments such as the following:

> When you use the term *derailment,* you are attaching moral judgments that associate higher value to higher status positions. That is, the principalship is better than the assistant principalship and the superintendency is better than the principalship. There are leaders who occupy so-called subordinate positions: They do a fine job, and they have no interest in positions held by superordinates.

We agree that there are persons for whom this is true and we affirm their value. We believe, however, that the term *derailment* applies to them if it is their desire to keep their present position and they are relieved of it. And if they don't want a position with higher status and pay—and aren't assigned to it—we can't say they have been derailed.

Our research on educational leader derailment has led to an interesting finding. Respondents can quickly identify the major reasons why educators they know have derailed, but when asked about their own derailment, they tend to balk. Blind spots in others are easy to identify; blind spots in one's self are given this name because they are literally true: We don't see them in ourselves. A common response to the question of derailment is, "Now that I have identified leadership flaws in others that have led to their derailment, I won't make the same mistakes." We have identified this as the halo effect (Brubaker, Simon, & Tysinger, 1993).

Because of the difficulties in *knowing thyself* and identifying one's own blind spots, Chapter 2 consists of a self-assessment in which you are asked to respond to a derailment checklist. This may serve as a pretest before you acquire a knowledge base on derailment, and it may also be useful as a posttest after you have read and tried out ideas in the book. The self-assessment inventory is in two parts: Checklist A is for those of you who want to become assistant principals and those who are presently assistant principals and principals; Checklist B is for readers who are superintendents or want to become superintendents. Although there are some common items in the two inventories, the roles of principal and superintendent are sufficiently different to warrant two checklists.

Chapter 3, "What Causes Educational Leaders to Derail?" discusses ways in which you can get off track. Examples of derailment have been culled from survey responses completed by assistant principals, principals, and central office leaders. In our original study, prior to the first edition of *Staying on Track* (1997), we surveyed 250 school and school-system leaders across the United States, with 150 current and aspiring superintendents keeping journals that yielded important information and attitudes (Brubaker & Coble, 1995). One hundred central office leaders (excluding superintendents), principals, and assistant principals were asked to answer the three following questions in writing:

1. Please keep in mind an assistant principal you know who has derailed. In your opinion, what was the primary reason for his or her derailment?

2. Please keep in mind a principal who has derailed. In your opinion, what was the primary reason for his or her derailment?

3. Based on your observation of others who have derailed, what are your concerns about your own derailment potential?

The following definitions of derailment were provided on the survey instrument. Assistant principal derailment: An assistant principal *who wants* a principalship does not live up to the expectations of the superintendent, the school board, or both, and therefore plateaus or is assigned a lesser position. Principal derailment: A principal *who wants* a so-called better school does not live up to the expectations of the superintendent, the school board, or both and therefore plateaus or is assigned a lesser position.

The first wave of research was followed in the new millennium by a series of individual and small group interviews, feedback from discussion groups, and leadership seminar participant responses. Practitioners who participated were included from the following states: Alabama, Florida, Georgia, North Carolina, South Carolina, and Ohio. The responses came from K–12 administrators who served in small and large schools; rural, urban, and suburban districts; and both racially diverse and not so racially diverse populations. In other words, these responses came from a cross section of administrators who represent schools as we know them in America.

The original questions were expanded to include the following queries:

- Why was the administrator who derailed a success in the first place?
- What do you consider to be potential accountability/high-stakes testing derailment factors?
- What strategies have you considered for avoiding derailment associated with accountability/high-stakes testing?
- What skills do you think are most important for enhancing data-driven decision making, improving student achievement, and increasing test results?

Respondents' answers to these questions are contained in Chapters 3 and 4 of this second edition of *Staying on Track*. You, the reader, will probably find it interesting to compare and contrast reasons why you think educators derail with causes of derailment cited by those we surveyed, and your responses to the self-assessment checklists in Chapter 2 will help you to do that.

Once you have read about major causes of derailment in Chapter 3, you will probably feel challenged to identify and implement antiderailment strategies, the focus of Chapter 4. This chapter begins with an assessment of what you have already done to avoid derailment, perhaps without giving much attention to it. Strategies others have used successfully will also be discussed. One of the major findings in our staying-on-track seminars is that there are a number of assistant principals, principals, central office leaders, and superintendents who can profit from our ideas even though they may never derail. They are not in enough trouble to derail, yet they can become significantly better leaders than they presently are. Their professional growth and development in our seminars is most heartening to themselves and us.

Your more general understanding of derailment strategies will be followed by Chapter 5, "Professional and Personal Plans for Development." The tools in this chapter will help you formulate a specific plan that will serve as a map for avoiding derailment or dealing with it if it happens. We strongly believe that professional development is a promising vehicle for reaching school and school-system goals. Educational leaders have to *get* at a high level in order to *give* at a high level, which is another way of saying that the learning of school leaders is as important as the learning of students (Sarason, 1972).

It is interesting to note that superintendents acknowledge that professional development is important, yet they need considerable help in giving attention to it. A comprehensive study of Ohio superintendents' perceptions supports this conclusion: "Thirty-six percent (36%) of the superintendents indicated that 'Staff Development' was something they should be doing but didn't have time to do" (O'Callaghan, 1996, p. 130). It is our intent to provide ideas and materials that will help superintendents, other central office leaders, principals, and assistant principals meet the challenge of giving quality attention to the professional and personal development of leaders.

Chapter 6, "Preparing Teacher Leaders for Tomorrow's Leadership Positions," focuses on an important matter in today's schools: shared decision making that gives teacher leaders an important role in the shaping and maintenance of school culture. We will give attention to the changing context in which educational leaders make their decisions. We will project ourselves into the future with an eye on barometers for change—those changes in schools that tell us something about changes in the larger society (Sarason, 1996). It is the transactions between schools and other institutions in our culture that are most telling. We will argue that proper attention given to teacher leader education today will pay rich dividends tomorrow.

Chapter 7, "The Seasons of an Educational Leader's Career," is a capstone chapter designed to help you, the reader, revisit where you have been in your career with an eye on where you want to be and can be in the future. Career path stories of practicing administrators will guide you on your journey. We urge you to draw upon understandings gained in the first six chapters of this book to plan your future in education.

The reader will note that the Prologue to this book is a cautionary tale about a school and school-system administrator who makes his way along a challenging career path. His story may be particularly useful to you in considering your past and planning for your career path in the future.

Before we list our references, we include a number of resources to help you deal with the derailment issue. They may be used in the following two major ways: (1) for you as an individual as you read this book and (2) for you as a staff development leader in a number of large- and small-group settings. One section of these resources takes the form of case studies, which may be thought of as the next best thing to being there. The format for these cases is as follows: A provocative case will be followed by a selection of alternative responses, after which the best possible rationale for each response will be given. We will also give what in our judgment is the best answer. You are urged to revise this format in any way that meets your creative impulses, thus making the cases your own. The reader is advised throughout the book to refer to particular resources relevant to ideas in the text.

We are interested in what you experience when you read this book. Please write us at the following e-mail addresses: dlbrubak@uncg.edu and lrrycble@bellsouth.net

Acknowledgments

In reviewing the correspondence with persons associated with the publication of this book, it is clear that it takes a community to give birth to a book. Kylee Liegl, Acquisitions Editor, had faith in a second edition and served as an advocate each step of the way. Her editorial assistant, Nadia Kashper, is on top of the details so essential to authors' efforts. Kristen Gibson, Production Editor, always brings excellence to her work. We always know that, when a manuscript reaches her, it is in good hands and the book will be completed with taste and elegance. Anyone who has authored a book knows the important role that a first-rate copy editor plays. We were fortunate indeed to have Stacey Shimizu bring her many talents to this role.

A special note of appreciation is given to hundreds of leadership seminar participants who reacted to our ideas and answered our survey questions. Several of these educators read this book in manuscript form and made suggestions important in the revision process.

Roberta E. Glaser
English Language Arts Department Chair
St. Johns Public Schools
St. Johns, MI

Michele Pecina
Principal
James Monroe Elementary School
Madera, CA

Mariela A. Rodriguez
Assistant Professor
Department of Educational Leadership and Policy Studies
University of Texas at San Antonio
San Antonio, TX

Dana Salles Trevethan
Principal
Turlock High School
Turlock, CA

About the Authors

Dale L. Brubaker is Professor of Educational Leadership and Cultural Studies at the University of North Carolina at Greensboro. He also served on the faculties of the University of California at Santa Barbara and the University of Wisconsin at Milwaukee. He received his doctorate in social foundations of education from Michigan State University. He is the author or coauthor of numerous books on education and educational leadership, including *Creative Curriculum Leadership* (1994, 2004), *The Hidden Leader: Leadership Lessons on the Potential Within* (2005, coauthored with Larry D. Coble), and *The Charismatic Leader: The Presentation of Self and the Creation of Educational Settings* (2006).

Larry D. Coble is Managing Associate with School Leadership Services, a division of The Coble Professional Group, a leadership and management consulting organization, and Director of the Collegium for the Advancement of Schools at the University of North Carolina at Greensboro. He provides speeches and seminars on leadership nationwide. He was a Senior Program Associate at the Center for Creative Leadership and served as assistant principal, principal, and superintendent in school systems in North Carolina. His most recent superintendency was in Winston-Salem, North Carolina. He received his doctorate in educational administration from the University of North Carolina at

Greensboro and is author of *Lessons Learned From Experience: A Practical Developmental Source Book for Educational Leaders* (2005) and coauthor of *The Hidden Leader: Leadership Lessons on the Potential Within* (2005, with Dale L. Brubaker).

Prologue

A Cautionary Tale

W e begin this book with a cautionary tale—a day in the life of an educational leader, the day Don found out that the board of education no longer needed or wanted his services as superintendent of schools. (Don is a composite of several superintendents we have interviewed.)

Until the past several months, Don had lived what may be described as a charmed life. Fifteen years ago, he started his first teaching job in a small high school. The first day at school, he almost instinctively did something that surprised even himself: He sat down at his desk and wrote, in large print, *Donald S. Brown, Superintendent of Schools.* Somewhat puzzled at this bold move, Don thought back to why he became an educator in the first place. He was actively involved in athletics, student government, and social activities while a student in high school. One of his coaches, who later became a superintendent, took a real interest in Don and encouraged him to become a teacher. This male superintendent was certainly a role model for Don.

Don got his first teaching job in the high school where he did his student teaching. His principal, aware of Don's interest in and potential for administration, gave him unofficial assignments around the school that prepared him for an assistant principalship. For example, Don supervised the parking lot in the morning and after school and handled some discipline situations. After three years of teaching, Don was assigned an assistant principalship in a junior high school, where he served for two years. An elementary school principalship came open, and Don, despite his reluctance to be an administrator at a level where he hadn't taught, accepted the position and was considered a quick study, with high credibility among his staff.

Two years later, the high school principal retired and Don was named the new principal. After two years on the job, Don succeeded the superintendent of schools, who took early retirement for health reasons. At this time, Don began work on his doctorate in education at a nearby university. This gave him an instant support system outside the school system and a place to express and hear the ideas and feelings of administrators in similar positions. It also introduced Don to new ways of looking at leadership. He was especially interested in the *know thyself* theme within educational leadership courses. He had been primarily task oriented in making his way up the ladder and had taken little time to be introspective. He shared the following in a letter to one of his professors a few weeks after his first semester of doctoral studies:

> I enjoyed your class this last semester and have been reflecting on your book and my personal and professional life. I qualify that statement with "sometimes," because you well know that this reflective thinking can be very uncomfortable at times. I get so intent on managing a school system and trying to get everything done that I lose sight of what's important— wanting to be where I am, and the importance of my relationships with others. One of the "curses" of my experience in administration is that I don't take much time to reflect— thank you for reminding me how vital that time is.

In doctoral study, Don was introduced to critical theory, with its emphasis on critique and the injustices society can impose on its citizens. Mainly, Don came to understand the interactions between the inner self and context. He was surprised that some of his easy solutions to societal problems, such as "All you have to do is pull yourself up by your bootstraps," were mechanisms that supported his extreme optimism and denial of how much some people struggle to keep body and soul together. The gift to Don in the early stages of this transformation was that he was less judgmental and self-righteous. The challenge was that he lost some of the comfort and security that come with thinking that he could control people and situations in his own interest.

Don's 4-year stay in this system as superintendent of schools was by all accounts highly successful. His outgoing and personable leadership style gave him high scores among students, teachers, other members of the staff, parents, and members of the community. Don also inherited a very talented central office staff that had a sense of vision as well as a sophisticated assessment system for administrators, teachers and, students. One of his assistant superintendents had a doctorate in educational research. Richard Jaeger was her advisor and, through his mentorship, she was given the opportunity to study under Michael Scriven, John Hattie, and Robert Stake. Consequently, when federal and state legislation was introduced, Don's assistant superintendent was able to keep the best of the assessment system she and her staff developed while at the same time accommodating new accountability mandates and high-stakes testing requirements. In short, she knew her stuff, and Don, once again a quick study, learned the language and procedures of evaluation and measurement. Both Don and his assistant superintendent kept the school board up-to-date on such matters.

After four years as a superintendent, Don received an offer to become superintendent of a large urban school system in the state. He did this despite recent knowledge in doctoral study about the average tenure of urban superintendents—2.5 years (Renchler, 1992)—in contrast to the mean tenure for large and small districts combined—6.47 years (Glass, 1992).

Don was initially elated with his new assignment. A few months into the superintendency, however, he experienced a sense of loss about leaving his previous school system that really surprised him. In fact, he felt blindsided by this empty feeling. He discovered, in conversations with his wife and colleagues in doctoral study, that he was not alone in having this feeling after accepting a new assignment. They too went through a brief feeling of depression in their new positions. Informal discussions helped Don see that he felt this sense of emptiness for not having completed the job he started when he had promised others he would continue into a second term.

A split board had released the former superintendent at the end of his four-year contract. Don had the full support of five of the seven board members during his first year—his honeymoon period. He was aware, however, that his position was vulnerable when two of his supporters on the board were defeated at the polls and two outspoken conservatives replaced them.

At this time, the board meetings became heated over a number of controversial issues: sex education, magnet schools, charter schools, redistricting, and the use of the high school by clubs whose agendas disturbed special interest groups in the community. Don did his best to achieve consensus on difficult issues, but one issue was not negotiable in his value system: the resegregation of the school system, something that was the result of magnet schools, the placement of new neighborhood school buildings, and the community's reluctance to engage in busing for desegregation purposes. Don was outspoken about his views on integration and desegregation in statements to the press and on television.

Unlike in his former school system, Don inherited a central office staff that had completely decentralized the assessment of teachers and students. Don's predecessor was a relatively weak leader whose principals thrived on the power bases they built. They gave little attention to the assessment of teachers and students, and some even engaged in testing irregularities that led to one principal's being forced into early retirement. As the state and federal governments became more active in mandating accountability measures and high-stakes testing, the central office tried to catch up with acceptable assessment systems. Several schools in the system were placed on probation by the state, and the local newspaper and television station had a field day with test results released by the state.

Don's wife and two children began to feel hostility from some members of the community, and crank phone calls in the middle of the night had his family anxious for their safety. At this time, an investigative reporter wrote a scathing article about what were claimed to be Don's financial practices. The article pointed out that the superintendent placement services that the board employed, what the reporter called "headhunters," had in turn been hired by Don as consultants to align the curriculum after he became superintendent. The reporter also uncovered the fact that Don served as a consultant for this placement and consulting firm on occasion.

At this time, Don and his wife had their first encounter with the reality that "bad things can happen to good people." Their third child died of Sudden Infant Death Syndrome (SIDS). Until this time, Don had been "on the arc of optimism." His worth was defined in his own mind by performance-based acceptance: He felt his worth depended on his acceptance by others. He had "jumped through the hoops" or "gone over the hurdles" in a highly efficient way, with promotion following promotion. Don realized that he had been conditioned to be reactive and analytical. He didn't know how to get in touch with his feelings, but instead was everything to everybody but himself.

With the convergence of the loss of a child at home and the possible loss of his position as superintendent of schools in a large urban system, Don felt he was on a downward spiral. His impulse was to work faster and harder, something that had worked to his advantage in the past. But in the process of following this impulse, he found it difficult to focus and at times felt a kind of claustrophobia in stressful meetings. Cynicism entered his life and conversations. Before, he had talked about the necessity of risk taking and the excitement of "living on the edge." He now said on occasions, "Being a leader makes it possible for people to hate you." And he somewhat humorously said that administration is "being responsible for irresponsible people . . . who seem to be having a lot more fun that you are having." In short, Don was fatigued from overwork and conflict, and some of his basic assumptions about his leadership in particular and life in general were being seriously challenged. Don reminded himself that some of his best classes in doctoral study taught him that one of the things that happens when a person changes is that he or she feels there is an inverted world order: You start to look at things as if they are upside down.

The church Don and his family attended was assigned a minister whom Don came to respect as a pastor and friend. A message new to Don was being preached from the pulpit: "You are loved for who you are, not simply what you do." Don was reminded of a leadership class in his doctoral study that made a distinction between spiritual power and political power, a point driven home by Don's reading of M. Scott Peck's *The Road Less Traveled* (1978) and Gloria Steinem's *Revolution From Within* (1992). Don's new minister repeatedly reminded the congregation that one's doing is but part of one's being, and who we are consists of many things that are not necessarily visible to others in what we do: our potential and basic assumptions about reality. For example, Don realized that defining our worth by simply getting the approval of others is a dead-end street; our doing is important but not all-important.

Don recognized that looking good through high standardized test scores and appearing to be a winner by bringing in grant money are not enough. Creative leadership is not getting people to do what you want them to do, regardless of whether they want to do it: Rather, creative leadership is using your talents to help others identify and use their talents and, in the process, trying to achieve worthwhile goals and objectives. Don sensed with every fiber of his being that he was involved in a struggle that had no easy answers—a struggle symbolized in two dreams he felt demonstrated the difference between his "old self" and his "new self."

When Don graduated from college and began his upward career ascent, he had a dream that grew out of his experiences living in a three-bedroom house as a child. He described the bathroom in this house as never having a cold seat because his mother, father, brother, sister, or grandmother always seemed to be in the bathroom when he needed to use it. Grandma was a special problem, as she liked to take hour-long baths. Don's dream was that he had just built a beautiful five-bedroom, three-bathroom house in the suburbs and was now challenged to find the very best furniture, carpeting, and so on to furnish the place. Don loved this dream, had it repeatedly, and shared it with those close to him who found it quite amusing in the telling—especially because Don and his family now had such a house in his second superintendency.

Don's new dream, which he had had only two or three times, was far less romantic and was, in fact, disquieting. He dreamed that their two children had left home and that he and his wife had purchased a smaller house that had already been owned by other occupants. The home was messy, and no matter how much Don and his wife tried to make the house like a new home, they couldn't turn it into a perfectly clean new house with everything in its proper place. Don and his wife laughed about these two dreams and how their efforts to control everything with their lives in general and their children in particular simply hadn't worked. Given the depression both Don and his wife were experiencing at this time in their lives, they humorously referred to themselves as "Numb and Number." (In fact, seeing the humorous side of things made them understand that they were slowly working themselves out of this state of depression.)

It is with this background in mind that we return to the day when Don received word that his services as superintendent of schools were no longer needed. Actually, receiving word wasn't exactly how it happened. Following the seething article, along with staff and community knowledge of the increasingly strained relationship between Don and his board, rumors of Don's impending firing began to circulate—first among staff and then in isolated pockets of the community. As it turned out, Don's opposition on the board had been talking out-of-school about their views that the superintendent was going to have to go. Had it not been for a call-in radio talk show, Don would have been totally blindsided. However, when a telephone guest inquired as to the truth of the rumor that the superintendent was going to be fired, Don's phone rang off the hook for the next hour and a half.

Fifteen minutes into the frenzy of calls, Don summoned one of his two most trusted staff members, Margaret Kahn. Margaret said that she had heard rumblings among some top staff a few days earlier, but had completely dismissed them as rumors. She indicated that, due to all the stress Don was undergoing on the job, she simply saw no need to burden him with what she was certain was a rumor. Now, they both knew that with this much smoke, there had to be a fire somewhere.

Don didn't have to wait long. Shortly before noon, Don received a call from his very supportive board chair, who appeared to be devastated. Jim Fick had just been told by one of Don's critics on the board that he had acquired enough support in the last week to not only not renew Don's contract, but also to buy out his final year. Furthermore, the critic requested an executive session for Thursday night, just two days away, to discuss this with the entire board.

The rest is history. What followed was a Thursday night executive session of the board in which three of Don's seven board members couldn't believe their ears about the criticism of Don's work and three were in such an emotional state that they would have written personal checks to get the superintendent out. The seventh board member could have gone either way, but with her political support base tied to Don's critics, and with this being an election year, she cast her vote to terminate. Don was called into the executive session and advised that in a few minutes the board would go into public session and place him on administrative leave until the details of his contract buyout could be worked out.

Don was told to remove his personal belongings by 5:00 p.m. the next day. Talk of legal fees, emotional wars, and staff, family, and community unrest proliferated in the area all day Friday and over the weekend. Sunday's newspaper headline read, "School Board Fires Superintendent." The amazing but predictable post-firing discussions never included anything about Don's alleged incompetence as a practicing administrator. Emotions ran high, however, when his views on maintaining racially integrated schools entered the discussion. The community split on this issue, and Don's value system left him without a job and him and his family in emotional upheaval. (Rarely does an intellectual issue lead to derailment in the superintendency; however, emotional and political conditions usually expedite the process.)

Don and his wife had such mixed feelings when the dust settled and they entered the buyout year. They appreciated those loyal friends who had supported them through one of the most difficult times in their lives, and they remained angry with those who had wanted Don's termination. Losing the job was for Don like the death of a friend: He didn't know how to grieve. His relationship with his minister was helpful, and this friend, realizing the extent of Don's depression, helped him get help from a professional therapist, a counseling psychologist. Fortunately, Don had maintained his health coverage as part of termination negotiations. During this time, it crossed Don's mind that he might have to leave home for a brief period of time to have around-the-clock psychological support, but this didn't come to pass. His therapist helped Don see that he had developed coping skills during the past few years that in fact kept him from making real and necessary changes in his life. Don recognized that he occasionally had the "false flu," and allergy attacks had become more and more prevalent. On occasion, he would be bedridden for two or three afternoons a week.

During this year, Don realized that completing his doctoral program was a godsend. It gave him structure, a goal, and a support network of professors and students. Most important, it gave him an arena away from his former school system in which he could be successful. The buyout year was a year of reflections and action, a year during which Don and his family could decide what to do next.

The story of Don's derailment raises several questions that may stimulate discussion:

1. What mistakes did Don make and what would you have done to avoid these mistakes? (We refer to this as the *personal face* of derailment.)

2. What did you respect or admire about Don's decision making in this career path story and why?

3. What mistakes did the school system make in relating to Don and what would you have done to avoid these mistakes. (We refer to this as the *organizational face* of derailment.)

4. What did you respect or admire about those in the school system, including board members, as they related to Don in this narrative and why?

5. What vocational options are now open to Don, and what advice would you give him and why?

Your answers to these questions make it clear why we introduced this section by calling it a cautionary tale: Staying on track is an important goal for the person (in this case, Don), for others, and for the organization as a whole. The educational leader who proceeds with caution must be alert and prudent. It is our aim in this book to help you develop these qualities of leadership.

Note: See Cases 1 through 5 in the Resources section at the end of this book for a discussion of issues related to Don's journey from assistant principal to superintendent.

CHAPTER ONE

Accountability and High-Stakes Testing

Lee Shulman: At the heart of my work on good teaching is the notion of a teacher as an enlightened, passionate intellectual.

Carol Tell: Do you find that this notion goes against the trend these days to measure the success of students—and their teachers—by standardized test scores?

Lee Shulman: The confusion stems from valuing standards, on the one hand, and embodying those standards in high-stakes assessments, on the other. The assessments end up corrupting the value of the standards. The standards get modified to be consistent with what we're able to measure in a high-stakes assessment. We have to ratchet down the standards and squeeze out all of the creative diversity because we want to be able to develop scoring keys that nobody can complain about or challenge.

C. Tell (2001, pp. 6, 8)

Standards, even when well implemented, can take us only part way to successful large-scale reforms. It is only leadership that can take us all the way.

M. Fullan (2003, p. 16)

Current realities with regard to teacher and administrator accountability in general and high-stakes testing in particular are so important in the culture of today's schools that we have added a special introduction to this subject in the second edition of *Staying on Track: An Educational Leader's Guide to Preventing Derailment and Ensuring Personal and Organizational Success.* This chapter will provide you, the reader, with a skeletal outline of the accountability/high-stakes testing situation in which assistant principals, principals, central office leaders, and superintendents find themselves. The material in this introduction provides vital information for getting the most benefit from the chapters that follow. Chapter 2 has self-assessment checklists that call for your responses to particular behaviors that often lead to derailment. Chapter 3 describes the causes of educational leader derailment, and Chapter 4 presents antiderailment strategies. Chapter 5 helps you construct personal and organizational plans for improvement.

Although our main focus in the present chapter will be on administrator accountability and high-stakes testing, the effect of this pressure on teachers is inextricably related to school and school-system leadership as well as to derailment issues. A major resource for this chapter is the seminal research and writing of R. Murray Thomas in his recently published book, aptly titled *High-Stakes Testing: Coping with Collateral Damage* (2005). By *collateral,* Thomas means attendant or parallel damage. His book has a special kind of credibility, as he is not an antitesting advocate but has instead considerable experience and expertise in assessment practices and test construction. His concern "is not about testing itself but, rather . . . about badly constructed tests, the improper administration of tests, harmful uses of test results, unrealistic standards of performance, and a lack of attention to evaluation methods other than tests" (Thomas, 2005, p. 10).

Advocates of accountability measures in general and high-stakes testing in particular argued that the following benefits would emerge. The achievement gap between the "haves" and the "have-nots"—primarily children of color and children from low-income homes—would be narrowed. Expectations for the "have-nots" would be realizable, thus stimulating teachers to do their best to reach such children. Traditional generalizations about students from good homes being successful and children from low-income homes being unsuccessful would be challenged rather than simply accepted. Teaching communities would be constructed to reach important goals with collaborative teaching and learning serving as an important vehicle for raising student achievement. Scores would go up as students and faculty discovered they could overcome what were previously felt to be obstacles. An argument for the No Child Left Behind Act (NCLB) of 2001 was that it would force many districts, principals, teachers, students, and communities to examine their areas of weakness in regard to addressing the educational needs of all students. As might be expected, however, research findings on such matters are mixed, with critics focused on collateral damage.

Professor Thomas (2005) cites four levels where administrators must apply their coping strategies: (1) national, (2) state, (3) district, and (4) the individual school.

THE NATIONAL LEVEL

Pressure at the national level is felt primarily from the alliance of the political party in power and the U.S. Department of Education as evidenced in NCLB. On January 8, 2002, President Bush signed NCLB into law. This act is the most significant reform of the Elementary and Secondary Education Act (ESEA) since it was enacted in 1965. The major stated purpose of NCLB is to narrow the achievement gap between middle-class white students and disadvantaged and minority students. The four basic emphases of NCLB are (1) stronger accountability for results, (2) more flexibility and local control, (3) greater options for parents, and (4) best teaching practices.

The two main kinds of collateral damage that evolved are "diminished public faith in the *No-Child* plan and resentment at federal intrusion into states' rights" (Thomas, 2005, p. 148). Meddling and inadequate funding eroded the credibility of those national politicians who mandated the program.

A major example of meddling that received tremendous media attention in January of 2005 was the disclosure that the Bush administration had paid Armstrong Williams, a prominent black media commentator, $240,000 to plug its education policies to minority audiences. Williams was expected to produce ads that featured Education Secretary Rod Paige and that promoted Bush's NCLB law. Williams apologized for his mistake in judgment, but said that he did not break federal law that bans the use of public money on propaganda. His critics disagreed.

Although polls of voters show enthusiasm for testing, "tests—and the sanctions that kick in when too many students fail them—are unpopular with Republican conservatives, who see No Child Left Behind as an unnecessary federal intrusion" (Kronholz, 2005, p. D5). Democrats who supported NCLB criticized President Bush for inadequate funding. State legislators caught "political flak when thousands of their schools didn't meet federal achievement targets" (Kronholz, 2005, p. D5).

One of the best critiques of NCLB was written by Norman Mailer in *Parade* magazine on January 23, 2005:

> NCLB would call for an unholy emphasis on doing well in tests. This could produce a narrowing of educational goals. Answers to true-or-false or multiple-choice questions would become the drill and the ability to write essays might fall to the side. That was bound to aggravate another weakness: High school students were showing reduced interest in books. (p. 5)

Mailer goes on to write about the importance of concentration in an activity such as reading. The ability to read depends on the desire to read. Furthermore, the constant interruptions in commercials in television programs every few minutes erode students' ability to concentrate and encourage obesity as children head to the kitchen for snacks.

In an effort to stem the tide of criticism of federal involvement in high-stakes testing legislation, the U.S. Department of Education sent members of their staff on appeasement missions. Specific criticisms remained with "states and local districts' complaints that the federal government has (a) underfunded obligatory programs, (b) set unreasonable test-performance standards for disabled and limited-English pupils, and (c) imposed unreasonable annual test-score targets, particularly for schools that enroll large numbers of children from economically disadvantaged homes" (Thomas, 2005, p. 149). A major criticism of the federal government's role in high-stakes testing is that it has mandated a one-size-fits-all approach to curriculum formation and evaluation methods. In fact, "when accountability and standards were first introduced without much knowledge of how best to implement standards . . . , leaders accomplished little other than alienating the better teachers with unhelpful intrusions" (Fullan, 2003, p. 6).

The role of teachers unions in relation to federal legislation in general and to NCLB in particular is especially interesting. The unions are opposed to NCLB, arguing that this arbitrary and capricious measurement of teacher performance is simply wrong-headed. "No other interest group can match [the teacher unions'] political arsenal. It is not surprising, then, that politicians at all levels of government are acutely sensitive to what the teachers unions want" (Moe, 2005, p. A12). At the end of February 2004, then-Education Secretary Rod Paige called the 2.7-million-member National Education Association a "terrorist organization" after the union criticized the implementation of NCLB (Thomas, 2005). His comment was made at a meeting for the nation's governors at the White House. Afterwards, Secretary Paige apologized for using inappropriate words.

It is clear that the education secretary has a good deal of power to set the tone in relating to various constituencies and to use discretionary measures. For example, Education Secretary Margaret Spellings, who succeeded Secretary Paige, has been willing to work with state and local officials in some ways that are quite different from her predecessor. She is committed to balancing states' rights to control schools with the federal government's responsibility to reduce the achievement gap between suburban white and urban minority students. She has especially listened to criticisms of NCLB by Republican politicians.

Terry Moe, a senior fellow at the Hoover Institution and a professor of political science at Stanford University, argues that the unions simply want to further their own interests: more spending, higher salaries, smaller classes, more professional development, and so on. "There is no evidence that any of these is an important determinant of student learning" (Moe, 2005, p. A12). Union contracts, he argues "are filled with provisions for higher wages, fantastic health benefits and retirement packages, generous time off, total job security, teacher transfer and assignment rights, restrictions on how teachers can be evaluated, restrictions on non-classroom duties, and countless other rules *that shackle the discretion of administrators* [italics added]" (Moe, 2005, p. A12).

An anonymous reviewer of the second edition to *Staying on Track* argues that Moe's attack on teacher unions doesn't tell the whole story: "While much of what Moe says is true, administrators also benefit from union-negotiated contracts. Administrators have higher wages, fantastic health benefits and retirement packages because of union activities. Administrators also have the ability to be more flexible with their time than teachers since they put in so many hours."

THE STATE LEVEL

Each state, according to NCLB, is expected to create standards for what a child should know and learn in reading and math in Grades 3 through 8. These standards are expected to drive the curriculum. Once these standards are set, student progress and achievement are expected to be measured annually according to state tests in a way that is consistent with state standards. Test data on each school should be publicly announced in an annual report card. Tests are to be designed to give each teacher, school administrator, and parents data about each student's progress. Policy makers have access to these data to assess student and school success and failure. Under the provisions of NCLB, each state has the responsibility to determine what students should learn in each grade. Students who fall behind are expected to have access to special resources such as tutoring and summer school.

Administrators at the state level have been heavily involved in high-stakes testing to the extent that some educators believe that state departments of public instruction have simply become testing centers. Their coping strategies have, according to Thomas (2005), included the following:

(a) furnishing extra help to low-scoring schools, (b) providing fix-up teams for failing schools, (c) identifying improvement factors, (d) advocating a growth model, (e) preferring states' own evaluation systems, (f) reanalyzing school-performance data, (g) adopting alternative tests for special students, (h) urging Congress to abolish the testing law, (i) delaying the increase in standards, (j) fudging cutting scores, (k) not reporting failing schools, (1) granting waivers, and (m) altering teacher-qualification rules. (p. 151)

The question remains, "How will the U.S. Department of Education determine whether states have met NCLB standards and assessment requirements?" A peer review process involving experts in the field of standards and assessments will evaluate state assessment systems against NCLB requirements. In short, the peer review process will be used to examine characteristics of a state's assessment system in relation to NCLB requirements. Direct examination of a state's academic standards, assessment instruments, and test items will not take place. Instead, the peer review process will examine evidence compiled and submitted by each state to demonstrate that its assessment system meets NCLB requirements. A state may use criterion-referenced assessments and assessments that yield national norms in its academic assessment system if they are used in accordance with Department of

Education guidelines. The peer review team will write a consensus report based on its examination of the evidence submitted by the state. The role of the state in organizing this evidence is obviously an important one.

Federal government officials in the U.S. Department of Education are often viewed by officials in state Departments of Public Instruction as outsiders determined to impose their will on the bureaucratic rung below them. School district administrators, in turn, often view officials from the state Departments of Public Instruction in a similar manner. In the process, the quality of the fix-up bureaucrats is often questioned by those below them. When large numbers of students fail tests, "students become discouraged, more drop out of school, and schools suffer punitive sanctions" (Thomas, 2005, p. 152).

THE SCHOOL-SYSTEM LEVEL

School-system administrators feel they are the third rung in the high-stakes testing bureaucracy. Many school systems had in place sophisticated assessment programs before NCLB was mandated. As a result, school-system administrators felt the new evaluation system imposed on them was a step down. Confusion was added to this matter when school-system administrators felt they were getting contradictory mandates from the federal and state governments. "If the results of federal and state testing standards are reported separately, parents can be confused about which report is the more valid whenever there is a discrepancy between the two" (Thomas, 2005, p. 154). In some cases, "schools are judged unsatisfactory under the federal plan but not under a state program" (Thomas, 2005, p. 154). It is then left to school-system administrators to try to reconcile these discrepancies.

Local assessments or a combination of state and local assessments can be used if they demonstrate that their system has a rational and coherent design. What does this mean? It means that the school system must identify the assessments, indicate how this assessment plan is aligned with the state's academic content standards, and demonstrate how information regarding student progress is related to the state's academic standards. The state must be able to defend the local assessments system when the peer review team visits the school system and determines if the local assessments system is consistent with NCLB guidelines.

Many school-system administrators feel that too much emphasis on reading and math has crowded out subjects such as the arts, social studies, and languages. In one district, other problems emerged as district administrators tried to align district standards with state standards. The state had set broad learning goals and had constructed tests to judge how well students were meeting them. The district then created a curriculum and a series of classroom tests to be sure that students were moving toward the achievement of state goals. Critics of these alignment procedures argued that the curriculum was shrunk to fit itself. In other words, only what was measured got done. Teachers taught to the test, thus limiting learning to only those items relevant to it. District tests were formatted to match state tests. Playing the testing game was especially pronounced on the part of beginning teachers, who were anxious about surviving in a highly competitive environment. Some teachers left teaching because of externally imposed standardization of curriculum and instruction. They felt that their professional judgment was replaced by politicians' mandates as translated by testing people in the state department of education (Brubaker, 2004).

Another problem, according to critics of the new mandates, is that high-stakes testing brings out the worst in competitive educators, some of whom turn to one or more "testing irregularities"— a euphemism for cheating. In some cases, a school's overall scores are raised by excluding certain children. A central office testing coordinator and a few teachers in one system were forced into retirement and an assistant principal was fired because of such alleged behavior.

THE SCHOOL LEVEL

School administrators, teacher leaders, and teachers are in the organizational culture where high-stakes testing takes place. They have to respond to critics' charges that standardized tests are too hard or too soft. NCLB requires a percentage of students at each school to score at grade level on state tests. Principals, or those who assist them, must disaggregate students by race, socioeconomic status, handicap or ability, and so forth to determine if subgroups are meeting requirements. Schools that repeatedly do not meet these goals must offer transfers to other schools or additional tutoring. With time, some teachers and administrators can be replaced and the school restructured. In North Carolina, a pioneer in the testing movement, critics say the statewide testing system is too soft. The standards were initiated 12 years ago. In the 1980s, the state legislature revamped its standard curriculum, and the ABC's accountability program was introduced in the 1990s to see how well the schools taught curriculum materials and how much students learned. What is meant by grade level is simply not clear, critics say.

Teachers and their administrators, particularly in low-income areas, often complain that their schools "focus narrowly on 'basic' academic skills, testing and discipline. The student boredom and academic failure that follow prompt calls for yet more testing and discipline" (Rabkin & Redmond, 2005, p. A9). It is also said that excessive attention to reading and math crowds out the arts. It is certainly true that at the heart of NCLB are the requirements that each state develop academic content and student achievement standards in reading/language arts and mathematics and an aligned assessment system that measures student achievement toward meeting those standards in each of Grades 3 through 8 and once in Grades 10 through 12 by the 2005-2006 school year. Some educational leaders have met this challenge by finding ways to integrate the arts into the basic academic program. "A study of 23 arts-integrated Chicago schools showed test scores rising up to two times faster than in demographically comparable schools. A study of a Minneapolis program showed that arts integration has substantial effects for all students with the greatest impact on disadvantaged learners" (Rabkin & Redmond, 2005, p. A9). It is also claimed that student progress and learning extend beyond test scores and basic subjects, so that students acquire higher-order thinking skills and feel more motivated to learn.

Michael Fullan (2003) points to a major problem that has emerged in the accountability and high-stakes testing movement:

> In the 1990s, when some systems (still the minority) began using better knowledge and investing in capacity-building training of principals and teachers, there were some basic improvements, for example, in literacy and mathematics. But because these strategies were tightly orchestrated from the center, principal and teacher ownership—the kind of ownership that would be necessary to go deeper on a sustained basis—did not exist. (p. 7)

CONCLUSION

The purpose of this chapter has been to provide a skeletal outline of accountability and high-stakes testing pressures on school-system and school leaders. These pressures obviously influence the leaders' ability to stay on track and avoid derailment. You, the reader, will see in the following chapters how these matters play out in the professional lives of assistant principals, principals, central office leaders, and superintendents. School and school-system leaders who are aware of the key issues surrounding accountability and high-states testing and who have a well-reasoned plan for dealing with these issues will enhance their chances of staying on track and avoiding derailment. Leaders who do not will be a performance risk to themselves and the systems of which they are a part. Our challenge throughout this book is to find ways to create a culture of caring and excellence while at the same time dealing with matters of accountability and high-stakes testing.

Note: See Resources A through E at the end of this book for a discussion of issues related to the challenge mentioned at the end of this chapter.

CHAPTER TWO

Self-Assessment Checklists

Reflection is nothing less than an internal dialogue with oneself. It is the process of bringing past experiences to a conscious level, analyzing them, and determining better ways to think and behave in the future.

—R. Barth (2003, pp. xxi–xxii)

The first thing to recognize about the importance of self-assessment is that a person does not operate in reality, but instead operates on the basis of his or her map of reality. Someone said that King George III was out of his head, to which a wag responded, "But it's the only head he has."

Second, what a person chooses to exclude from his or her map of reality is as important as what is included. We call this *negative affirmation:* We affirm the goodness of a limited number of choices by narrowing the universe of possible choices. An example of this is one we have all experienced. It is late Sunday evening and we are returning from a vacation, anxious about going to work the next day. We stop at the nearest supermarket, one we have never been in before in our lives. We quickly make our way around the store to pick up a select number of items, such as bread, milk, and cereal. We are able to do this efficiently because our map of the territory tells us what not to look for in various parts of the supermarket. We also know where to look for items that we desire. A conceptual framework based on past experiences serves as a map for negotiating the territory.

Third, only when we are open to change in our map of reality can we decrease our chances of derailment. In the process, we celebrate those parts of our map that have worked for us in avoiding derailment. In other words, change and conservation go hand in hand.

The following checklists will help each of us identify behaviors that often lead to derailment. *Checklist A* is for readers who want to become assistant principals and those who are presently assistant principals and principals. *Checklist B* is for those who are superintendents and those who aspire to the superintendency. Please check those behaviors that you perceive as existing in your educational leadership. Items checked are those you will especially need to give attention to in order to avoid derailment. Also, please check statements with which you agree—items that may well lead to derailment. Leave blank those statements with which you disagree. Checklist items are organized according to major themes: incompetence, external political conflict, internal political conflict, difficulties with leadership processes, diminished desire to learn and improve, legal and/or moral problems, and personal reasons. We encourage you to be honest in your responses for the sake of your own growth and development. Your responses are for your own eyes only unless you wish to share such responses with another person or persons. (Note: Statements in Checklists A and B were developed based on the authors' research and interviews with current school and school-system leaders.)

CHECKLIST A

Assistant Principalship and Principalship

1. Incompetence: not equipped to carry out major role functions

   ❑ 1.1 I find it difficult to take the initiative and prefer to be directed by someone else.

   ❑ 1.2 I often feel indecisive.

   ❑ 1.3 I have good intentions but poor organizational skills.

   ❑ 1.4 Follow-through is a problem for me. I am often given assignments that I fail to complete.

   ❑ 1.5 I often look good but fear that I have little depth or substance.

   ❑ 1.6 I have difficulties with the "table manners of leadership"—such as entrance rituals that relax and welcome people and exit rituals that leave visitors with a good feeling after being with me. Civilities are not my strong suit.

   ❑ 1.7 I worry about being articulate in general and am afraid that I sometimes use poor English.

   ❑ 1.8 I want as much "life space" as possible and will spend as little time as possible in the school to which I am assigned.

   ❑ 1.9 I may well have a difficult time making and implementing tough decisions. Disciplining students may well be my Achilles heel.

   ❑ 1.10 I am not comfortable with instructional technology in general and computers in particular. I will simply find ways around this lack of knowledge.

   ❑ 1.11 My ability to understand and interpret test results is inadequate.

   ❑ 1.12 I have difficulty in using test results to develop improvement plans.

   ❑ 1.13 I am reluctant to seek help from the central office in disaggregating test results and helping teachers develop and use instructional strategies.

❑ 1.14 My ability to explain students' test results to parents is inadequate.

❑ 1.15 I am not on top of test security issues in my school.

2. External Political Conflict: difficulties in relating to people and organizations outside my school

❑ 2.1   Nonalignment with the philosophy of my super-ordinate(s) may well be a major problem for me.

❑ 2.2   I tend to be outspoken and political to the point where it may get me in trouble with superordinates.

❑ 2.3   I sometimes come across as too self-confident and opinionated, which some people read as my being an authority on everything.

❑ 2.4   I am knowledgeable and not afraid to show it, which may make my superordinates look out of date.

❑ 2.5   I take things personally and sometimes talk about my school in a negative way outside the school.

❑ 2.6   If warranted, I will criticize central office staff in public.

❑ 2.7   If things go wrong in my school, my superordinates should take the heat. After all, this is what they are paid for.

❑ 2.8   I have no interest in nor will I participate in "good ol' boy games"—like going to lunch, attending football and basketball games, going out for drinks after the games, and so on.

❑ 2.9   It will be in my interest to invest time and money in the reelection campaigns of school board members.

❑ 2.10 I will do a good job in my school, but spending time getting to know and participate in the culture of the community is a waste of my resources.

❑ 2.11 I am ill prepared to relate to the teachers' union.

❑ 2.12 I tend to be indiscreet about privileged information.

❑ 2.13 The way I dress is my business and quite frankly none of the business of my superordinates.

❑ 2.14 Standardized test scores are of little interest to me, but I will show the flag and seem to be interested in them.

❑ 2.15 My relationship with central office leaders on high-stakes testing matters is poor.

3. Internal Political Conflict: difficulties within the school

❑ 3.1 Credibility with my superordinates is all-important. My teaching staff didn't appoint me and they won't fire me.

❑ 3.2 I am willing to take an unpopular position on a controversial issue even if my staff doesn't support this position.

❑ 3.3 There are times when my staff in general and advisory council in particular will want me to support a position I don't agree with, but I probably won't do so and I will be irate if they go over my head.

❑ 3.4 Although my staff may be disturbed by my establishing a political base outside the school, I will do so to get promoted.

❑ 3.5 High test scores are the key to upward mobility, and I will do whatever it takes, short of cheating, to get them up.

4. Difficulties With Leadership Processes: poor judgments at critical times

❑ 4.1 I have difficulties in formulating the projecting vision for our school.

❑ 4.2 Faculty deliver when they are afraid. All of this positive reinforcement stuff simply pampers them at the expense of a well-organized school.

❑ 4.3 It is inevitable that a leader plays favorites. It goes with the territory.

❑ 4.4   Involving faculty in school decision making is a waste of time. The principal is in charge of the school and shouldn't have his or her power eroded.

❑ 4.5   Communication skills are of little importance if you simply do your job. Staff members know what they are expected to do without my communicating my expectations to them.

❑ 4.6   Reading people well is not part of the principal's job description and is highly overrated. The assignment of people to leadership positions is a low-level priority.

❑ 4.7   You can't make changes too fast. A job needs to be done and done quickly, so do it.

❑ 4.8   Teachers don't need the involvement of principals in classrooms.

5. Diminished Desire to Learn and Improve

❑ 5.1   One you get to know the job, you should give your resources to it rather than attending staff development workshops. You really can (and should) do the job at this point on automatic pilot.

❑ 5.2   There is nothing wrong with being more interested in retiring than in learning. After all, I have paid my dues and others can now pay their dues.

❑ 5.3   I know that I frequently behave in such a way that I send to others the message, "I don't want to be here."

6. Legal and/or Moral Problems

❑ 6.1   As I look around me, I find little evidence that assistant principals can be derailed for legal and moral problems.

❑ 6.2   An assistant principal or a principal should do a good job and give little attention to legal and moral issues, because they take care of themselves.

7. Personal Reasons

❑ 7.1   Personal reasons for derailment are of little consequence for me. They are simply not likely to be an important consideration.

❑ 7.2   The way to get ahead is to get a doctorate. After getting this so-called union card, it will be easy to find better employment.

❑ 7.3   It is simply not necessary to push my present employer to save my present position for me upon my return from doctoral study.

CHECKLIST B

The Superintendency

1. Strategic Differences With Management

☐ 1.1   People are people and school board members are school board members. If I have a good personal relationship with them, political matters will play a secondary role.

☐ 1.2   As superintendent of schools, positional authority rests with me. Sources of power, such as expertise, charisma, and succorance, are overrated. It is still true that the head of the organization can accomplish what needs to be accomplished. Followers respect a leader who has an agenda and isn't afraid to push it.

☐ 1.3   The way to deal with the media is to try to avoid them—especially television.

☐ 1.4   Some people say that today's organizations have to be more open to public scrutiny. However, the smart superintendent, the kind I respect, gives out information on a need-to-know basis.

☐ 1.5   The power of the religious Right is highly overrated as to influencing local boards of education.

2. Problems With Interpersonal Relationships

☐ 2.1   Superintendents who have demonstrated their intelligence with good grades, particularly during graduate study, are likely to be good at interpersonal relations.

☐ 2.2   Some people use the term *micromanagement* in a disparaging way; but to keep people in line with your vision and be sure that they do quality work, you have to check on their progress or they will slack off.

☐ 2.3   Interpersonal relationships are important but highly overrated in gauging the effectiveness of superintendents. The important thing to note is that the effective superintendent is task oriented and gets the job done efficiently.

3. Difficulty in Making Strategic Transitions

❑ 3.1 Some people say that there are defining moments or critical incidents that make a real difference in superintendent effectiveness. But, in fact, this is not true. The superintendency consists of one undramatic moment after another. It is your staff's job to know this and efficiently carry out their day-to-day tasks in a predictable way.

❑ 3.2 My understanding of the accountability movement in general and high-stakes testing in particular is inadequate.

❑ 3.3 Accountability and high-stakes test results are my responsibility as the buck stops with me.

❑ 3.4 I have difficulty in explaining to the public in a simple, straightforward manner the meaning of accountability and high-stakes testing.

❑ 3.5 Principals should understand that if something can't be measured, it shouldn't be included in curriculum and instruction.

4. Difficulty in Molding a Staff

❑ 4.1 The best way to relate to a member of your staff who was a candidate for the superintendency is to forget the past, don't discuss this matter with him or her, and go about your business.

❑ 4.2 The work of an organization is done through its formal structure. The key to your success as a superintendent is to use this formal structure to your advantage.

❑ 4.3 A superintendent is wise to put aside any fears related to the role of leader. Hard work is its own reward because you don't have to think about yourself or the *know-thyself* philosophy you hear about in higher education.

❑ 4.4   My inclination is to monitor staff in getting the job done. Why fake it by pretending I am someone I am not? I'll be authentic even if a few critics criticize me for looking over their shoulder.

5. Lack of Follow-Through

❑ 5.1   Follow-through is often overrated. What is important is to highly motivate people and trust them. Then follow-through won't be a problem.

❑ 5.2   Paperwork and other scut work forced on the superintendent from the state Department of Public Instruction and others will always be overwhelming. The trick is to identify those assignments that are meaningless and then simply not do them.

❑ 5.3   Staff members don't have to be part of a team to get scut work done. In fact, they tend to waste their time talking to each other when they are close together. Simply give them their assignments and try to put them in autonomous workstations to get their work done.

6. Overdependence

❑ 6.1   The board of education must be pleased or you won't survive as a superintendent. Some may call it overdependence but, in fact, the effective superintendent knows that the board is calling the shots.

❑ 6.2   Boards of education understand that it is the responsibility of the superintendent to make personnel decisions that they rubber-stamp.

CONCLUSION

In the following chapter, we will use the checklists you have responded to in this chapter as an outline for our discussion of the major causes of educational leader derailment. We urge you to return to your responses to the checklist so that each of your answers is placed in larger context. In fact, you may wish to photocopy your self-assessment responses so that you can place them side by side with the outline for discussion in the next chapter.

CHAPTER THREE

What Causes Educational Leaders to Derail?

It has taken us nearly a century to discover that, as a form of organization, bureaucracy lacks the tools to manage complex work, handle the unpredictable, or meet distinctive client needs.

—L. Darling-Hammond (1997, p. 66)

The present chapter is organized according to the two self-assessment checklists you recently completed in the previous chapter. Checklist A included items for readers who either want to become or are assistant principals and principals. Checklist B contained items for educational leaders who aspire to the superintendency or presently hold this position.

CAUSES OF ASSISTANT PRINCIPAL AND PRINCIPAL DERAILMENT

In surveying assistant principals, principals, and central office leaders, we were surprised at the degree of uniformity in their responses as to the causes of assistant principal and principal derailment. We have categorized these responses in descending order of frequency as follows: (a) incompetence, (b) external political conflict, (c) internal political conflict, (d) difficulties with leadership processes, (e) diminished desire to learn and improve, (f) legal and/or moral problems, and (g) personal reasons.

Incompetence

Incompetence was defined succinctly by one respondent as "not [being] equipped to carry out major role functions." Occasionally, a person assigned to an administrative position fails to take the initiative and instead wants to be directed by someone else. Such an assistant principal or principal seems to have backed into the position, wants the perks and salary, but simply fails to assume the role of leader. So-called good ol' boy principals, for example, have traditionally expected a lead teacher to provide leadership in the areas of curriculum and instruction (Brubaker, 2005). Indecisiveness leaves followers with the feeling that things won't be done or won't be done well. As Father Theodore Martin Hesburgh, president of the University of Notre Dame from 1951 to 1987, said, "The very essence of leadership is you have to have a vision. You can't blow an uncertain trumpet" (quoted in Austin & Brubaker, 1988, p. 104). Dennis Moser (2005), a seasoned principal, adds, "Being the leader in a community means being willing to be the torch bearer, to be the one keeping the fire going" (p. 17). The effective leader leads by example—for example, by having substance, knowledge, a strong work ethic, and a positive attitude toward what should and can be accomplished.

It is also interesting, with regard to a principal's leadership in curriculum and instruction, that he or she may overrate his or her leadership in such matters. Barnett Berry, a professor at the University of South Carolina, surveyed 150 principals and 900 North Carolina Teaching Fellows who had graduated from their respective institutions of higher education. North Carolina Teaching Fellows receive complete funding for their four years of higher education in exchange for a four-year teaching commitment after graduation. "More than 90 percent of the 150 principals surveyed said they talk about instruction frequently with their teachers. But only 43 percent of the Teaching Fellows thought they had frequent discussions with their principals about instruction" (Simmons, 1995, p. 1). This survey also found that "only 43 percent of the Fellows felt they could influence curriculum—the heart of any classroom education. Almost 80 percent of the principals, however, said teachers influence curriculum" (Simmons, 1995, p. 1). This once again supports the power of the halo effect: Principals feel they are more competent than others; or, as in this case, the best and the brightest of beginning teachers think such principals are.

Another sign of incompetence, according to several respondents is the lack of organizational skills. Problems with follow-through were frequently cited: As one respondent said, "He was all talk and no action. He didn't meet superordinates' timelines and was always late in handing in reports. He dressed well but had no substance. We referred to him as 'the empty suit.'"

Administrators who are long in marketing themselves and their schools but short in delivering on their promises are suspect: "Ordinary schools are busy convincing themselves and others how excellent they are; great schools know that they are not as good as they can be" (Glickman, 1990, p. 68).

Some assistant principals and principals show their incompetence by not having the so-called table manners of leadership (Brubaker, 2005). Said one interviewee, "People are not relaxed around our principal because he is brusque and bullies faculty. He doesn't know how to greet people and see them out of the school with a good feeling. He uses poor English, which sets a bad example for the staff and children." (See Resource B, "Entrance and Exit Rituals," in the Resources section at the end of this book.)

A fairly common criticism of some principals is that they simply aren't in the building enough. "We have a ten-minute principal," an assistant principal relates. She adds, "He is here for five minutes each morning to greet the students and five minutes each afternoon when they get on the buses." Some assistant principals and principals look for any excuse to be somewhere between the school and central office. (See Case 2, "Assistant Principal Expected to Run School," in the Resources section at the end of this book.)

Occasionally, a principal or assistant principal is perceived to not be tough enough to handle difficult situations. "We have some rough discipline situations in this school," a principal related, "and the assistant principal doesn't project the strength to maintain discipline." It should be added that schools vary with regard to degree of toughness.

A sure sign of incompetence these days is an administrator's lack of knowledge about technology in general and computers in particular. Fifty percent of Ohio superintendents surveyed in early 1996 indicated that it is extremely important that students be provided access to up-to-date computers and other scientific technology (O'Callaghan, 1996, p. 78). We may assume this percentage is higher today. In some cases, principals and superintendents will not be as technologically current as those they lead. Effective educational leaders will identify colleagues with such technological expertise, learn all that can be learned from these experts, and include them in appropriate leadership teams. These experts are often *excluded* from such teams, due in part to the special language associated with various technologies. Such experts sometimes have a tendency to assume others have the expertise they have and also attempt to teach others in a fast-paced and somewhat impatient manner. Principals, superintendents, and central office leaders must make every effort possible to identify and support those with technological expertise who can translate difficult ideas so that all can understand what should and can be done in this important area of communication.

Teachers and administrators face the reality of accountability in general and high-stakes testing in particular. One principal exclaimed, "How do we deal with the fact that many educators have a negative attitude toward accountability and some act as if the mandate doesn't even exist?" She continued, "The accountability movement is testing our leadership performance as principals beyond belief!" Another principal in this small-group interview added, "My teachers cringe when they hear the word 'accountability,' and the stress associated with attempts to raise test scores has depleted our energy and enthusiasm." She continued, "The pressure is increasing, our ability to respond is decreasing, and burnout is just around the corner."

One veteran principal candidly admitted, "Some of us can only do a fair job of understanding and interpreting test results, but we really lack the ability to use this information to develop improvement plans." A fellow principal said, "I am reluctant to seek help from the central office in disaggregating test results and helping teachers develop and use instructional strategies as they are really busy." As the discussion continued, it was clear that this principal felt it would be an admission of weakness to seek help from the central office.

A beginning principal shared her observation that the parents of high-achieving students pay more attention to test scores than parents of low-achieving students. She said to us, "I have not had experience in talking to parents about the meaning of testing and test results in my preservice education at the university or in our professional development workshops." A colleague talked about some of the contradictions she faced in talking to adults outside of the school: "Last year, the students in my school made a significant gain on the average when all students were calculated, but showed a big decrease in the number of students who met minimum standards. How do I explain this to the news media and parents without appearing to be on the defensive?" Another principal added, "Although I have really tried, I cannot figure out how the federal No Child Left Behind legislation dovetails with my state's accountability program." These comments opened the floodgates of frustration other principals in the group felt: "When will politicians wise up and involve school teachers and administrators in developing accountability legislation and standards? Also, if some of these state and federal mandates were implemented first on a trial basis, we would not have so much confusion and frustration."

Test security issues are often discussed among principals and assistant principals: "There should be a zero tolerance for misuse of tests to improve test scores. Test security and ethical use of test items should be of utmost importance." "Using statistics to either enhance or downplay test performance is not acceptable. In an election year, watch out for those who will use accountability in the schools for political, rather than educational purposes."

External Political Conflict

External political conflict was defined by respondents as difficulty in relating to people and organizations outside the school. During his interview, Fran Nolan (2005) looked back at his early experience as an assistant principal:

> I simply didn't know how attentive a leader has to be to politics. I hid behind moralisms and didn't realize until I had power that you don't have it. That is, you have to trade fragments to the point where you can't keep score: "Who do I owe what?" (p. 1)

(See Case 4, "New Superintendent Edges You Out of Position," in the Resources section at the end of this book.)

Nonalignment with the philosophy of superordinates was cited by several respondents as a major cause of derailment. An experienced principal describes difficulties in adjusting to a new superintendent and board of education after a merger: "*In this new system, a principal is only one bad decision away from derailment. I appeared not to fit in because I had reservations about new leaders' vision for my school and the school system.*" If this principal is outspoken and considered to be too political, he will be in trouble with his superordinates. If he is articulate, he may come across as arrogant. And, if he is knowledgeable and not afraid to show it, he may well make his superordinates look out-of-date. He will cross the line into insubordination if he publicly criticizes the direction in which his school, the school system, or both are moving.

It is important that an assistant principal or principal accepts responsibility or takes the heat when things go wrong in the school. This may even mean that the school administrator will take the blame for errors made by his or her superordinates on occasion. This is one reason why assistant principals describe themselves as "leaders in the middle."

It is common knowledge that some presidential candidates will choose less qualified vice presidential candidates simply because they feel more comfortable around them. Who wants to spend a lot of time with someone who makes you nervous? One way in which assistant principals and principals establish an affinity connection with their superordinates is to go to lunch, meet in athletic contexts, or something similar, after which they have drinks together. Engagement in these activities has commonly been a source of power for "good ol' boy" administrators who share the so-called macho ethic (Brubaker, 2005). A principal described a colleague in a rural system who failed to participate in these activities: "He didn't play the good ol' boy game. He was more interested in poetry than in sports. He cared about others and was really different from most administrators in the system."

Some principals in the same rural system appeared to be more like politicians than educators. They routinely invested money in the political campaigns of school board candidates. If their candidates won, they were given special access; but if the candidates lost, they were punished. One principal consistently invested in opposing candidates' campaigns to hedge his bets.

Assistant principals and principals who fail to be in touch with the community outside the school risk a good deal. A survey of Ohio superintendents indicates that 53% of them believed it was extremely important to broadly engage the community in support of the schools, and 52% thought it extremely important to create partnerships with parents in educating their children (O'Callaghan, 1996, p. 78). The effective educational leader recognizes the benefits associated with establishing community partnerships and networking with all stakeholders to help strengthen the perception of an administrator who cares and has a vision of excellence. (See Resource C, "Working Alone and Working With a Team," in the Resources section at the end of this book.)

Respondents in the Midwest and Northeast cited difficulties in relation to the teachers' union as a potential source of derailment.

They felt ill prepared by their administrator preparation courses to deal with such matters.

Most superintendents are sensitive to schools with low test scores in this age of accountability and high-stakes testing. In many systems, such scores are published in newspapers, and real estate agents use schools with high test scores as a way of directing potential buyers to a particular geographic area of the school system and away from other areas.

One of the first things an assistant principal and principal learn is that "you have to watch what you say to whom." One must be sensitive to privileged information, and a lack of such sensitivity may quickly lead to derailment.

Finally, some superintendents give special attention to the dress of assistant principals and principals. A professional image is valued, and informal dress is considered inappropriate (Greene & Bentley, 1987). At the same time, some teachers, particularly in elementary schools and middle schools, want assistant principals and principals to participate in activities with children that call for informal attire. Once again, assistant principals and principals are persons in the middle. (See Case 3, "Principal Hears New Superintendent's Views on Dress," in the Resources section at the end of this book.)

Internal Political Conflict

Internal political conflict refers to difficulties of a political nature within the school. One of the real-life contradictions faced by the assistant principal and principal is that credibility with superordinates and school staff is extremely important, yet it is impossible to please both parties when some decisions are made. (See Resources D and E on contradictions facing educational leaders at the end of this book.) Some staff members will expect you to represent their views to central office leaders even when you disagree with such views. Central office leaders will, in turn, expect you to implement controversial positions that will erode your credibility with school staff members. In the event that you don't represent your staff to the central office, their representatives in school systems with shared decision making and flattened organizations may well go over your head to the central office and even to school board members. This occurred in an elementary school when teachers in one wing of the building didn't have adequate heat despite maintenance workers' efforts to rectify the problem. Teachers who were members of the school's advisory council sent tersely written memos to the superintendent and school board members, voicing their complaint. The principal and superintendent were outraged. The leadership team said that they were simply acting out shared decision-making rhetoric.

The assistant principal and principal interested in upward mobility face another contradiction. They will need a political support base outside the school in order to be promoted, but if they are too obvious in establishing such a base, they will look more interested in the next position than in their present one. If you are involved in upward mobility moves, you will need to know how the school system pecking order works. At the same time, you want to create community within your school. Dennis Moser (2005) describes the challenge:

> Students, teachers, parents, bus drivers, cafeteria workers, office staff, maintenance people, central maintenance people—all people associated with a particular school—need to feel ownership, commitment, and acceptance at a school. The connection ought to be non-conditional. You are connected because you are. (p. 11)

The trick is to be aware of pecking orders without reinforcing them. In fact, you will need to choose your battles carefully to challenge these power structures. Assignment of parking spaces, names and titles on doors and other conspicuous places, and introductions to staff members at meetings of parents are especially sensitive matters facing the assistant principal and principal.

Attention to test scores can be as important internally as externally. A respondent calls our attention to this: "Our principal was so consumed with gaining district reputation with high test scores that she lost the support of the faculty who felt she had set aside the school's child-centered orientations."

In short, the principal's credibility within the school depends on technical proficiency—the ability to do well what has become known as *administrivia,* such as scheduling—but such proficiency, even though it affords security, is not enough in itself because it doesn't assure connection. Moser (2005) speaks to this: "Connection and community have everything to do with tone and theme and human value and motivational and internal body clocks that wake us ready and willing for another day and another challenge" (p. 10).

The challenge a principal faces is to be able to be highly collaborative and still make the-buck-stops-here decisions when necessary. This is in contrast to the view that the principal must do what teachers say or make unilateral decisions. The principal who develops "radar" or "antennae" to maintain a constant feel of the tone, mood, and morale of the school will demonstrate the importance of assessment of the school culture—an essential ingredient of instructional leadership.

Difficulties With Leadership Processes

Difficulties with leadership processes refers to poor judgments by assistant principals and principals at critical times. As indicated earlier, the formulation and projection of a school vision leaves followers with the feeling that the leader has a sense of direction and knows what he or she is doing. One of the messages sent when a leader has a shared school vision is that there is something more important than satisfying the leader's ego needs. The opposite message is conveyed when the assistant principal or principal instills fear in the staff. Paranoia and a lack of trust are usually associated with such leadership. A few critical incidents or defining moments in a school's history symbolize such leadership-gone-wrong.

An elementary school principal was fed up with a number of problems that surfaced during the first few months of school. The pest control people had to be called in to kill bugs attracted to the remnants of food eaten in classrooms. A few teachers openly challenged the principal during the most recent faculty meeting, and the principal overheard criticism of himself when he entered the teachers' lounge. A week before Christmas, this principal went home and made a pitcher full of martinis. He then sat down at his word processor and began typing a memo to the faculty, knowing full well that this venting exercise would never actually be distributed to them. After his second drink, he finished the following memo.

December 18, 2004

To: The Faculty

From: The Principal

Re: Procedural Changes in the School

It has come to my attention that there are several matters that need to be addressed before our vacation begins. We have needlessly had to use part of our budget to bring in pest controllers because *some* of you have had food in your classrooms.

I know that you are stressed out because of the holiday season. You have presents to buy, food to prepare, and guests to entertain. However, *your problems at home must not create problems at school.* The faculty lounge has become a den of destructive criticism—a morale breaker for all concerned.

The following procedural changes will take place immediately:

1. No food will be allowed in classrooms. Food will be eaten only in the cafeteria.

2. Faculty members will use the faculty lounge one at a time.

3. Problems from home will not be the subject of conversations at school.

Have a good holiday!

The next day, the principal inadvertently took this memo to school on top of a stack of papers. His secretary, relatively new to the job, photocopied and placed the memo in faculty mailboxes. As happens in such matters, faculty members have creative and often humorous ways of naming such critical events. In this case, the memo became known as "The Christmas Edict."

Paranoia, a word commonly used by followers to refer to a distraught leader, can sometimes cause the assistant principal or principal to retreat to an area or activity that can be absolutely controlled. Respondents describe this in a number of ways:

> Our assistant principal in the high school simply had no people skills. He saw faculty decision making as a threat to his control. He was authoritarian and rigid. He began spending almost all of his time at his computer keyboard. Evidently, the principal was relieved not to have him wandering around the building blowing up at people and so he was left alone.

The playing of favorites among faculty and staff can be another way of losing credibility with them. In effect, the leader creates an in-group and an out-group. Honorifics and the giving of awards, such as Teacher of the Year, constitute another especially sensitive issue facing the assistant principal and principal.

Time and again, we heard about poor communication skills that worked to the detriment of the administrator and the school at critical times in its history. Teachers' roles are always negotiable to some extent, but they want to know what their leaders expect of them. It affords security even if they disagree with such expectations; it says, "I care enough about you to give attention to your role in this school." Dennis Moser (2005) provides us with insights about the significance of communication between the leader and followers:

> Creation of community means attention to people first, listening to the human concerns, acknowledging the emotion, the feel, and then taking action on something specific later. Sometimes people expect and need no action at all. They just want be heard. . . . We administrators sometimes make the mistake of trying to fix, trying to be too efficient, too active. People often just want to get the feel of what short of priority an issue is for the leader, not that anything is actually going to change right now or be done, but just to be heard. Teachers say to me over and over, "I just needed to talk." (p. 13)

Assistant principals and principals are sometimes derailed because of their inability to read people well. The wrong person is assigned to a leadership position and fails.

Poor personnel decisions, including hiring, also can leave people with the impression that the leader doesn't know what he or she is doing. High-visibility assignments are a mixed blessing. Occasionally, one meets a newly appointed assistant principal or principal who is overanxious and makes changes too fast. The problem is compounded when he or she refers to him- or herself as "a change agent," thus implying that others must change but he or she is not expected to do so. Followers react angrily if ignoring the leader's manic actions doesn't work.

Finally, a common complaint against some assistant principals and principals is that they spend little, if any, time in classrooms. One assistant principal comments,

> I shouldn't say this but teachers in our school refer to the principal as "The Ghost." He simply doesn't spend any time in classrooms but assigns all evaluation to assistant principals. His excuse is that he simply doesn't have time, but I suspect that he wouldn't know how to talk about curriculum and instruction even if he wanted to do so.

The effective educational leader recognizes the importance of leading with the heart and the head. The leader's ability to truly listen to the verbal and nonverbal messages of those who wish to communicate with him or her is a key to achieving a balance between leading with the heart and the head.

Diminished Desire to Learn and Improve

Diminished desire to learn and improve is another category for items relating to potential derailment of assistant principals and principals. Some leaders fail to avail themselves of opportunities to learn, as evidenced by the fact that they don't attend staff development sessions or, if they do, they act as if they are on automatic pilot.

Respondents cite a few assistant principals and principals who act as if they are more interested in retirement than in learning. One person in a leadership position held up three fingers every time he was frustrated. It symbolized the fact that he had three years until retirement. A respondent described such a leader by observing, "He acted like he didn't want to be here."

We will argue in the remainder of this book that it is the educational leader's desire to make sense of the world around him or her and what he or she experiences that makes a major difference in the quality of leadership given to the setting. It takes a learning leader to create a learning community in a school.

Legal and/or Moral Problems

Legal and/or moral problems are occasionally cited by respondents as reasons for derailment. A few assistant principals and principals are fired for criminal acts in violation of the public trust. These violations receive prominent headlines in local newspapers and are featured on the television news. Respondents cited the following as examples of legal problems: shooting a man in a nightclub, decorating one's house with artwork paid for with the PTA and state funds, shoplifting in a store, being arrested on morals charges involving a minor, and misappropriation of funds.

Although legal issues are often dramatic and clear-cut, moral issues are more subtle and difficult to analyze. One of the difficulties with moral assertions is that the person making them can leave others with the impression that "I am better than you." At the same time, assistant principals and principals are challenged to hold themselves to a high standard of behavior. Case studies at the end of this book focus on moral issues, and we urge you to read and discuss them.

Personal Reasons

Personal reasons are sometimes mentioned as reasons for derailment. A woman may leave an administrative position to have a baby and decide not to return as an assistant principal or principal, according to one respondent. Family problems are also cited as reasons for leaving an administrative post. On occasion, an assistant principal or principal will take a year's leave to pursue a graduate degree, only to find that his or her position has been taken by someone else and other similar positions are not available.

CAUSES OF SUPERINTENDENT DERAILMENT

Several studies in recent years have given attention to the increasingly high turnover rate of superintendents (Brubaker & Coble, 1995; Brubaker & Shelton, 1995; Hood, 1996; Hoyle, Bjork, & Collier, 2005; Lane, 2003). Hoyle (1988) predicted a 40% to 50% turnover rate by the year 2005 due to several factors, including retirement and derailment. His prediction has held true, and the media have given a good deal of attention to the high turnover rate of superintendents. Derailment of superintendents of schools is especially acute in our urban areas. (See Case 5, "What Kind of Superintendent Will I Be?" in the Resources section at the end of this book.)

In an effort to identify and understand causes for derailment, we read the journals of 150 current and aspiring superintendents across the United States who attended leadership seminars we conducted. We also reviewed related research and writing on the subject of superintendent turnover.

As with the derailment of assistant principals and principals, superintendent's perceptions as to why they left their positions vary to some extent compared to perceptions held by direct reports—those in positions close to superintendents (Hood, 1996). Variance can once again be attributed to the halo effect. That is, superintendents tended to see themselves victimized by outside forces, whereas direct reports were more critical of superintendents' leadership and located greater blame in the actions of such superintendents.

However, there was more commonality between the perceptions of superintendents and direct reports than we thought we would find. It is therefore accurate and useful to identify the following six categories of responses for superintendent derailment, in descending order of frequency: (a) strategic differences with management, (b) problems with interpersonal relationships, (c) making strategic transitions, (d) difficulty in molding a staff, (e) lack of follow-through, and (f) overdependence. (We hold the view that the degree of frequency on these matters is less important than the usefulness of categories and examples in stimulating thinking and discussion so that those interested in the cost of derailment can limit its occurrence.)

Strategic Differences With Management

Strategic differences with management means, in effect, strategic differences with the board of education. This comes as no great surprise at a time when people want an active role *in* government, not simply representation *by* government. In concrete terms, this means that school board members are often emissaries of special interest groups. They have definite agendas to advance and axes to grind. The result is that, intent on their own agendas, these school board members tend to micromanage school systems; they often can't see the big picture and they don't grasp how roles of administrators and board members should differ (Brubaker & Shelton, 1995).

Because of the power special interest groups hold over board members (and all politicians), today's leaders—unlike those of yesteryear—can't simply use their authority to elicit what they consider desirable actions from others. Instead, superintendents who are going to be effective in the age of the disposable superintendent must know how to use other sources of power, such as expertise, charisma, and succor (Brubaker, 2005). Some superintendents have made the transition in using nonauthoritarian sources of power in relating to board members, but others have not.

Superintendents and their management team members may say and do things that are no longer confined to one community. Think of the Alabama high school principal who had what allegedly were his views on interracial dating at an end-of-year prom—reportedly expressed during a school assembly—beamed throughout the world (Brubaker & Shelton, 1995). It is inevitable in dealing with such a volatile situation that the superintendent will be more vulnerable to disagreements with board members, and such disagreements will be immediately visible to the public because of television news.

Regardless of the wishes of superintendents and board members, organizations have become more open in letter and spirit. The public demands this. The prominence of special interest groups, such as the religious Right, has forced superintendents to either adjust or leave. Actions within the board represent vocal advocates who use their internal and external networks to push their agendas. In some systems, disgruntled ex-principals, who have themselves derailed, become school board members with one important agenda in mind: Get rid of the superintendent.

Problems With Interpersonal Relationships

Problems with interpersonal relationships are a major cause of superintendent derailment. McCall, Lombardo, and Morrison (1988) quote a college graduate who dramatically describes the shift from the culture of higher education to the culture of the work world and its demands on leaders:

> In college, I used my intellectual skills to get good grades by knowing the right answers. But at work, I found out that knowing the right answers was only 10 percent of the battle. Working with people was the other 90 percent. And we hadn't learned that at school. (p. 22)

Lack of communication and poor communication are repeatedly cited by people dissatisfied with a superintendent's leadership. Direct reports especially associate these difficulties with superintendents who can't seem to help themselves from micromanaging others. Rather than delegating tasks and giving staff the appropriate freedom to accomplish those tasks within a given time frame, the micromanaging superintendent is always in the face of those he or she has asked to do the task.

Though some hardy souls in the central office might be confident enough to confront this behavior and tactfully make their views known, the micromanaging superintendent will likely take a dim view of such "noise in the system." In short, the micromanaging superintendent simply communicates a lack of trust in the abilities of other educators to do their work. Micromanagers also tend to focus on too many matters at once, thereby squandering their resources.

Micromanagers often operate on the basis that information gathering is the one kind of intelligence that assures personal and organizational success. Daniel Goleman (2000) reminds us that our emotional intelligence—how people manage feelings, interact, and communicate—is a major key to effective leadership. This thesis is also reinforced by the research of McCall, Lombardo, and Morrison (1988).

Difficulty in Making Strategic Transitions

Difficulty in making strategic transitions is another major cause of superintendent derailment. (See Resource A, "Questions Important to Educational Leaders Who Want to Avoid or Deal With Derailment," at the end of this book.) A dramatic example of this occurs when the board of education makes an abrupt change in its membership. In one school system, a board that traditionally had African American representation for its large minority population lost this representation at election time. The newly appointed superintendent faced a board that had some members with notoriously racist attitudes. She also faced outspoken leaders in the African American community. Her solution: The superintendent created a high-level advisory group of African American leaders in the community who worked directly with her. At the same time, she made efforts to create consolidated support among board members to shape an agenda that wouldn't bring harm to any students in the school system. These efforts made some difference, but after two years in office, she resigned to take a university position. She saw a system that was resegregating itself, and knew that her choice was between self-derailment and derailment by the board.

Another superintendent saw the composition of the school board swing from liberal to conservative right before his eyes. The new board viewed shared decision making as a left-wing plot, and the struggling superintendent finally resigned in despair after losing his credibility with the new locus of power in the community.

Some veteran superintendents had difficulty in dealing with the transition from local accountability systems to new systems mandated by federal and state governments. A superintendent shared the following with us:

> We took great pride in the central office staff's assessment system. They worked with principals in a variety of ways to introduce innovative programs in curriculum and instruction, and these programs had student and teacher evaluation built into them. Our assessment people traveled to curriculum conferences with our principals to stay up on latest developments in curriculum and instruction. All of us resented federal and state mandates that were both inadequate and confusing compared to what we already had in place. None of us understand some of the federal and state guidelines. We just do the best we can to interpret and implement them.

A newly appointed superintendent told us that she made the mistake of thinking that she was personally responsible for all accountability and high-stakes test results: "I learned with time that this has to be a shared responsibility. Central office leaders, principals, assistant principals, teachers, and parents must share this responsibility. It is a team effort."

Another superintendent working on her doctorate in administration helped us see how important it is to communicate in a simple and straightforward way: "Much of my coursework in graduate school was in research and evaluation. I got bogged down in my communication with parents and the board of education in the language of assessment. This language was appropriate in higher education, but it was too sophisticated for my purposes of explaining accountability and high-stakes testing to parents and others."

One problem that many superintendents have inherited with federal- and state-mandated accountability and high-stakes testing is the exclusive use of the word "measurement." Measurement is but one kind of evaluation or assessment. Politicians and bureaucrats love numbers, because they can be used to claim credit when test scores are up and assign blame when they fall. One doesn't have to reflect too much to realize that a person's growth and development are not restricted to quantitative assessment. The superintendent who believes that if something can't be measured it shouldn't be included in curriculum and instruction has a very narrow view of curriculum, instruction, learning, and assessment.

Difficulty in Molding a Staff

Difficultly in molding a staff can force a superintendent to derail. A newly appointed superintendent may well find one or more high-level staff members who are not very happy about the new appointment. In fact, one of these leaders may have been a candidate for the position. A young superintendent shared his strategy for dealing with this situation:

> I made it a point to talk to my assistant superintendent, who was in the running for the job I got. I said to him that we should be able to share in an honest way how we felt about things, air these ideas, and then move on with our jobs in the interest of having a smoothly running system. He thanked me for making this overture and being so honest about it at the front end. With time, we not only had a good working relationship but also became friends.

A second superintendent told us a story about his entrance into a large rural system that had a less than happy ending:

> It became clear to me when I was on the job for a week or two that nepotism was rampant in this system and indeed in the state. Some central office leaders were related, and principals and assistant principals were part of the same inbred system. I took a stand early in my appointment that the best-qualified person for the job would be hired. In fact, I said this in my

interviews with the press and television newspeople. Malcontents turned to the deputy superintendent, a former candidate for the job I received, and thwarted me at every turn of the road. After two years of this harassment, it was obvious to me that I didn't have the power base to continue leading. Under pressure from the board, I resigned.

The nepotism cited by this superintendent is firmly implanted in some school systems. (See Case 4, "New Superintendent Edges You Out of Position," in the Resources section at the end of this book.) If you are not aware of the networks in place to support such nepotism, you can easily be blindsided, thus leading to your isolation and perhaps unemployment.

Hardworking and effective central office leaders, principals, and assistant principals are often offended by newly appointed superintendents who leave them with the feeling that the system has no history or no history of any value. Newly appointed superintendents can become so absorbed in their plans for the system's future that they make no effort to understand its history and culture. It is as if they have arrived at a party several hours late but act like it has just begun. A director of instruction shared with us her experience on this matter:

At the first meeting of the year with his central office staff, the new superintendent stood in front of us and said, "Welcome aboard!" I turned to a friend and said, "I thought it was our ship." The superintendent then said, "I've been told that there have been some serious problems in this system before I came. I want to put all of this behind us and don't want to hear anything more about them." After this meeting, my friend said to me, "We still have some grieving and healing to do about our past, but we sure won't do this in front of our new superintendent."

It is especially crucial that superintendents establish a working relationship with informal leaders who have a following in the district, our survey respondents say. This helps establish a shared commitment to a higher educational purpose.

The challenge of molding a staff into an effective leadership team was the secret fear of a prominent Virginia superintendent, Sue Burgess (1995). Unlike other women superintendents we've known, she knew from the time she began teaching that she wanted to become a superintendent of schools. When asked where this dream came from, Burgess said,

> When I graduated from Roanoke City Schools, we had a woman superintendent, Dorothy Gibboney, the first woman superintendent in Virginia. This was in the '60s. During my 12 years in the Roanoke City Schools, we had two superinten-dents—a woman and a man. If you had asked me at age 18 what percentage of superintendents in our country are women, I would have naively responded, "I guess about 50 percent." I didn't realize that Dorothy Gibboney was an anomaly. (p. 2)

She continues her story:

> The thing that kept my dreams alive is that if I really want to do something, telling me that I can't do it invokes a passionate response. My internal voice says, "I'll show him!" The earliest memory of this was when I was a fourth grader in beginning band. I took my brother's hand-me-down clarinet to school. Toward the end of the year, the band director approached me in private and said, "Sue, did you say you had a cornet or any other instrument at home that you could switch to? I'm sorry to have to tell you this, but you'll never be able to play a clar-inet." All summer, I kept my secret about his comment and in the fall, a miraculous thing happened! We got a new band director. When I went back to school to start the fifth grade, I walked in with my clarinet and didn't tell the band director I couldn't play. I pretended that I could play and worked even harder that year. By the time I graduated from high school, I was the only person from Roanoke who had been in the All Virginia Band four times. I went on to play in the Roanoke Symphony, the Winston-Salem Symphony and the Greensboro Symphony. (p. 4)

Sue Burgess was also discouraged by some educators from becoming an assistant principal, principal, and superintendent:

> During the 23 months that I sought a job as a superintendent, I applied 16 times. Six of those times, I was not selected for an interview. Of the 10 times that I interviewed, I was chosen as a finalist six times. On four of those six occasions, I was told informally that I had finished second. I started to get a "brides-maid complex," but like Avis I decided to try harder! I was especially frustrated over gender-related questions like the following:
>
> > How can a woman delegate and follow up to see that the job is done?
> >
> > How can a woman check the roads in bad weather to decide whether or not to have school?
> >
> > If there is a roof problem, how can a woman check it out?
> >
> > If you get this job, what will your husband do? (p. 6)

Burgess was persistent and kept her dream alive, but she was still disturbed by a secret fear that she shared with her husband after receiving her first appointment as a superintendent:

> My fear about becoming a superintendent did not have to do with technical knowledge. I wasn't really intimidated by having to construct a budget or learning about construction, finance, dealing with architects, or any other similar matters. I know that if I am motivated to learn something that I can! My secret fear centered around the difference between man-agement and leadership. I knew that I was a good manager, but I secretly worried how I would "get things done by others." My music background helped me at this point. The bandleader plays not a note himself or herself, but is responsi-ble and absolutely accountable for the way the band sounds. I knew that I had been a good principal. I knew that I could

do the job of director of instruction, but would I be able to get other persons to perform those roles without having to or wanting to do the jobs for them? Could I avoid becoming a micromanager? (p. 8)

Burgess has answered this question on the firing line. She has learned to give leadership to molding a staff by instruction, delegating, trusting, and teaming. In the process, she has received an offer to head a system 10 times larger than the first one she was hired to lead. She took this position, served well for several years, and then assumed another superintendency in coastal North Carolina.

Lack of Follow-Through

Lack of follow-through can be a major cause of derailment. Sixteen percent of Ohio superintendents surveyed believe that they spend too much time on noneducational matters, such as petty problems and complaints. Too much paperwork and time constraints were also cited by this group of superintendents. Ten percent cite unfunded federal mandates and state mandates as dislikes, and another 10% disliked resolving conflicts and pressures from parents, the community, and special interest groups (O'Callaghan, 1996, p. 55). The point of these data is that there are many real pressures that make it difficult for superintendents to follow through. Also, if you add to these woes the response of nearly 50% of Ohio superintendents—the difficulties of funding/finances/passing levies—you grasp the problem of adequate human and nonhuman resources facing these leaders (O'Callaghan, 1996, p. 119).

The secret to having good follow-through is to put together teams of people who get the job done. Once again, the superintendent who has the slightest inclination to be a micromanager is in trouble, because a lack of trust in the abilities of others teaches them to be hesitant. Followers always have to check with the superintendent, thus further eroding the superintendent's time as a resource.

Overdependence

Overdependence, particularly on the board of education as a whole or on a few board members, was cited as another major cause of superintendent derailment. A former superintendent, who has moved into university administration, shares the frustration she felt on the firing line:

> Due to the intensity of the job, you always know that burnout can be just around the corner. Until our governance system was restructured, I would deal with the loneliness and frustration of the superintendency, much of which is caused by how school boards function in this way: I would cry a lot with those with whom I really trust; I would try not to make any decisions; I would kiss up to the board and let board members make any hiring decisions they wanted to; and I would define my role as a maintenance person. As a result, I might get two contracts of four years each. (Brubaker & Shelton, 1995, p. 18)

The former superintendent might well have added that the price you pay for such a strategy is emptiness and cynicism—the death of hope.

CONCLUSION

There is a phenomenon with regard to derailment that sometimes puzzles observers: The very traits that helped a principal or superintendent climb the ladder turn out to be fatal flaws (Anders, 2005).

A school board searched for a superintendent who would bring life to a school system whose 20-year veteran superintendent was retiring. They felt they had the ideal candidate in a young leader who was poised, confident, articulate, passionate, comfortable in relating to the media, fond of the dramatic gesture, and experienced in moving from one important project to another. He was greeted with open arms by those who felt that high-energy change was precisely what was needed at this time in the history of the school system.

The new superintendent had a fairly long honeymoon period, during which many old-guard central office leaders and principals were nudged out of their positions. The board was pleased with the amount of money saved in a downsized central office, and the media described the new superintendent as a dynamic but financially conservative leader. During the third year of his superintendency, criticism began to emerge: "He's throwing out the baby with the bath—too many changes made too quickly." "Why does he always have to be the center of attention? He's a narcissist because it is always all about him! He marches around like a Pied Piper." "He created so many magnet schools that there is no rationale for most of them."

Changes in the board of education soon led to a split board that no longer supported the superintendent. The dynamic superintendent was released, and the board hired a veteran who was known for his ability as a healer. The context when he was hired and the context several years later were entirely different.

We want to end our present discussion of the major causes of derailment on a hopeful note. Certainly, there are important challenges facing today's assistant principals, principals, and superintendents—probably greater than at any time in our nation's history. The extreme optimism following World War II has been replaced by realistic hope. This is to say that things will not naturally get better but will rather depend on hard work by leaders who are competent and who care. Our survey and the survey of Ohio superintendents (O'Callaghan, 1996) indicate that educational leaders like best being in a position to implement both vision and good educational programs. They also like working with staff and community. Success experienced by teachers and students is important to superintendents and principals. Most educational leaders like the challenge of the job and being in a position to make a difference (O'Callaghan, 1996, p. 51).

In the following chapter, we will identify and discuss anti-derailment strategies—those concrete next steps that we can take to avoid wasting personal and organizational resources.

CHAPTER FOUR

Antiderailment Strategies

We have a deep tendency to see the changes we need to make as being in our outer world, not in our inner world. It is challenging to think that while we redesign the manifest structures or our organization, we must also redesign the internal structures of our "mental models."

—P. Senge (1990, p. xv)

As an educator, you are concerned about derailment from two perspectives: your personal derailment and the cost of derailment of others to the educational setting where you give leadership. It is simply common sense, therefore, that you can identify and implement antiderailment strategies that will enhance personal and organizational effectiveness.

Our research uncovered a number of insights that you might find useful as you ponder the matter of derailment. These insights are general in nature and are not listed in any particular order. We have framed our understandings about preventing derailment in the form of recommendations.

This chapter's introduction to antiderailment strategies will be followed by two chapters that spell out in specific terms how staff development can help administrators, teachers, and teacher leaders both avoid and deal effectively with derailment. Staff development in this case recognizes the role that organizations have played in causing derailment (the organizational face of derailment), as well as the role that persons have played in causing their own derailment (the personal face of derailment). Locating blame is less important than taking steps to help persons and organizations, schools and school systems, both avoid and deal productively with derailment.

THE RECOMMENDATIONS

Recommendation 1: Ask Yourself What You Have Done and Are Currently Doing to Avoid Derailment

The first step to avoiding derailment is to examine what you have done in the past—and are doing now—to avoid derailing. Listen also to others' assessments of their own effectiveness. Seeking and responding to feedback are crucial to a leader's success (Lombardo & Eichinger, 1995). The feedback won't always be good news. A trusted associate, for example, advised a superintendent, "You are so data-driven that you fail to realize that real change depends on persons rather than numbers." The superintendent didn't ask for, but profited from, this feedback.

Given the technical responsibilities of your job as an educational leader, it is challenging to take time to reflect. Yet it is precisely your ability to reflect that can help you avoid derailment. A reflective exercise we have found instructive is to ask educational leaders to focus on a person they know whose halted progression became a derailment. We then ask each educator to describe in detail a success story about this person, followed by the story of his or her derailment (McCall & Lombardo, 1983). The following four questions emerge from this exercise:

1. Why was this leader who derailed successful in the first place?

2. What events caused this leader's weaknesses to surface?

3. What caused this leader to derail?

4. How did this leader differ from others who continued to be successful? (McCall & Lombardo, 1983).

We will now take a look at one educator's responses to these questions so that you, the reader, can see how this four-part framework can be helpful.

Why was the principal who derailed a success in the first place? She had strong interpersonal skills, was trustworthy, had a strong work ethic and sense of commitment, and was willing to help others (i.e., she was a caring person).

What events caused her weaknesses to surface? She had poor conflict management skills and was unable to build support. She made bad political choices. The public perceived her to be a flawed leader. Internal political conflict emerged in her school and there were philosophical differences between this principal and her subordinates and superordinates.

What caused this principal to derail? Some of her conscious choices were received poorly by those she led. At times, she was too rigid, and at other times, she was too flexible. As a result of these difficulties, unanticipated consequences emerged.

How did this principal differ from others who continued to be successful? She was unable and unwilling to change or adapt. She switched from being more opinionated to being less opinionated. She tried to please too many people, something that caught up with her. She also did not make good use of feedback given to her. If much of this evidence sounds contradictory, it is because this is how others received her. They did not perceive her as comfortable in her own skin as a leader.

This reflective exercise portrait makes a number of things clear to participants. First, a person's success and derailment can't be separate from the life of the organization and vice versa. Second, a person's success at one point in an organization's history may be a cause of derailment at a later time in that organization's history.

Third, a person's strength can also be viewed as a weakness. Fourth, events that cause derailment are seldom dramatic, but instead are usually small and cumulative. Fifth, all leaders leave tracks from which we can learn. (See Case 1, "Getting on Track," in the Resources section at the end of this book.)

The assistant principalship and the principalship can be lonely positions. The nature of the work, which is characterized by as many as 1,500 brief interactions with others in a week's time, is by definition reactive. However, the never-ending demands, usually determined by someone else's agenda, should not suggest the absence of loneliness. (See Resource C, "Working Alone and Working With a Team," in the Resources section at the end of this book.)

There is a saying that goes this way: "It's lonely at the top, but it's not crowded." How you define the "top" depends on your perspective. Certainly, the chief administrators in a school are at the top in their particular setting. That there are few, if any, others in similar positions in your setting is what we mean by the top not being "crowded."

Building administrators are so busy, day in and day out, that they simply do not take the time to reflect. It is critical that you regularly set aside time for reflection. This may mean arriving at school even earlier than normal or it may mean staying late when the halls are cleared and you are there alone. The point is that you must be still and listen to that inner voice: "What did I do today— or this week, for that matter—that I can learn from? What worked for me? What got in my way? How could I have improved on my performance? Is the work truly meaningful? How can I learn more and at an even faster rate? What are the personal costs in terms of family and private time?" These types of questions will help developing leaders reframe their approaches to problem solving, avoid burnout, and ultimately prevent derailment.

Recommendation 2: Take Care to Create a Culture in Which Staff Members Feel Comfortable Entertaining Conflicting Ideas

Teaching-team leaders, assistant principals, central office coordinators, and superintendents are especially challenged to listen to the dissident voice. It is often from this voice that the educator learns the most.

The primary challenge that often goes with listening to the dissident voice is that when school leaders are given the opportunity to build their own teams, their first thought is to employ individuals who think in similar ways. This often guarantees quick compatibility and easy communication. However, the result of surrounding yourself with those who are similar to you in philosophy, perhaps loyal to a fault, and who are "yes" people is that it is too easy to fall victim of groupthink. Remember that the person who is truly loyal will tell you when you're headed down the wrong road.

We sometimes see administrators who inherit their team and do not have the opportunity to build their own. If there is a lack of compatibility early on, the leader in charge is already thinking, "How can I get this person transferred or out of my school or department?" This approach can be a mistake. In all likelihood, this individual would already have a good understanding of the culture and could be of great assistance in helping you, as a leader new to your position, read and assess the culture.

The key is to prize what can be learned as much as what can be managed. It is our enthusiasm for our work that keeps us from becoming cynical—the deadliest of leadership qualities. It is helpful to remember that one of the greatest gifts we can give not only to those we lead but also to ourselves is to build on the memory of what it was like to be a child. Curiosity and a sense of exploration drove us as children to learn everything we could about the world around us. We enhance our chances of learning more if we not only take the time to listen to the dissident voice, but also structure our approach to leading by regularly including the dissident voice.

Recommendation 3: Reflect on the Qualities and Actions That Helped You Reach Your Current Position

It can be useful to think about the steps you took as you ascended the career ladder so that you can capitalize on your ability to make good choices—a process that will tell you what you need to do in the present. Reflect also on the transitional periods in your career, those defining moments and critical incidents that led you to new understandings and new challenges. Positive images from your past can be inspiring in the present. With all the demands on administrators, especially with increased account-ability and high-stakes testing, it can be especially helpful to men-tally go back to a time when things were going very well for you and bring that positive mental image into the present. It is easy to focus on what has gone wrong and what is missing, to the detri-ment of what has gone right and what is there to capitalize on in the present and the future. It is a mistake to get stuck in a deficit model, where we pay interest on a debt we don't owe. (See Chapter 7 for a more detailed discussion of career stages.)

Recommendation 4: Accept the Necessity of Accountability

Accept accountability as a necessary requirement of schools and schooling and treat it in the same manner as any other impor-tant administrative function. Neither downgrade nor overempha-size student performance scores. Learn all that you can about the accountability legislation mandated for your school. Interpret this to your students, teachers, parents, and the public in simple terms. Present the facts with regard to school performance in a straightforward way.

Join other educators in promoting the concept of shared account-ability, which emphasizes that students, parents, legislative bod-ies, businesses, higher education, and industry are all responsible for the quality of the schools. Insist that you and your colleagues be provided training in the organization and interpretation of test data and how to use these data in developing school improvement plans. Support responsible groups, such as administrator and teacher organizations, the Parent Teachers Association, and school board associations, in discovering and disseminating the advan-tages and disadvantages of various mandated accountability programs. Be factual.

Strive to maintain a balanced instructional program in your school. Assure that your students benefit from and enjoy courses such as art, music, life skills, and physical education, which are not included in accountability testing. Create a winning culture in your school or schools.

Instill in those you lead your view that they are mature, responsible persons who always strive to do their best. Make parents a vital part of this winning team. Maintain a sense of humor and don't be afraid to laugh at yourself.

Recommendation 5: Build a Strong Support Base With Principals

School principals are extremely powerful individuals by virtue of their leadership responsibilities, their direct connection with parents and students, and the influence that they can exert with teachers. They are therefore among the most autonomous middle managers in our society. For example, alumni, especially at the high school level, have strong feelings of loyalty toward their school and much of that loyalty can be directly tied to the principal, especially one who has been in the role for a significant amount of time. Effective principals, who are viewed to be fair and who are able to get the job done, can become outstanding allies for the district office.

By choosing to include principals in the decision-making process and then asking them to support district-level initiatives, the superintendent and other district-level leaders are modeling the importance of empowering by level to get the job done. The fact of the matter is that high-quality principals make everyone's job easier.

Recommendation 6: Build Trust Throughout the Organization and Build Effective Teams When Needed

Trust depends on creating an affinity connection. Staff members will perceive you as authentic when you listen and follow through with concrete steps that assure others they have been heard.

Educational leaders are, in many ways, what they talk about. If you have a passion for curriculum, instruction, and learning, and talk frequently about these matters with others, your enthusiasm can be contagious. If you engage only in small talk, you might be well liked, but you won't be respected by teachers and others who are serious about education.

You will erode your credibility if you always insist on being right. M. Scott Peck (1993) speaks to the matter of pretension and rigidity: "Most of the evil in the world—the incivility—is committed by people who are absolutely certain that they know what they're doing" (p. 91). It's fine to be wrong sometimes, as long as you are a learner and willing to change. The high visibility of your position makes an apology a sign of strength, rather than weakness. It demonstrates that you have compassion and understanding.

One of the most visible signs of trust in an organization is the presence of effective teams. Effective leaders blend people into teams whose strong morale and spirit are evident to all. Open dialogue invites everyone to express opinions without feeling coerced and discounted. Team members are allowed and encouraged to finish and be responsible for their work, with success defined in terms of the whole team. Belonging to such a team is a reward in itself. Team members learn to manage conflict through listening and a sharing of their views. Tough agreements are reached as team members search for common ground. Creative ideas are invited, with team members translating their meaning so that those on the firing line can understand and implement such ideas. Teams can actually manage the vision and purpose of the organization's culture, thus inspiring and motivating members of the culture to do their best. Problem solving and the reconciliation of dilemmas play a key role in the life of a team. Some issues can be solved whereas others call for a team to do the best it can and live with the consequences. An honest analysis of the situation is necessary in both situations.

Trust can be difficult to attain and easy to lose. Work hard at extending trust to those you lead. Basic to this approach is granting the trust before it is earned. Realize that to be trusted, you must visibly demonstrate that you trust those under your leadership.

Recommendation 7: Work to Ensure Common Expectations

As a superintendent, meet and plan with the school board in a way that is consistent with your common expectations. As an assistant principal or principal, meet and plan with advisory boards in a way that is consistent with your common expectations. Our research indicates that there is frequent misunderstanding and lack of comprehension between such bodies when they have substantially less information about strategic issues than you do.

One of the first leadership acts in which a superintendent should engage is to jointly meet and plan an agenda for the board's expectations. This is true if the superintendent is new to the district or if the superintendent is a veteran of the district who gets a "new" board. This joint planning session allows for a common understanding of the board's priorities and sets the direction for the district under the current board. Failure to engage in this activity can result in superintendents who are confused about the board's expectations and can give board members with special interest agendas an opportunity to advance their individual concerns without the benefit of full board support.

Principals and assistant principals who make meeting with their advisory boards a priority are demonstrating a commitment to keep communication lines open, and they are showing that they care enough about what their advisors have to say to listen. The act of meeting, listening to, and responding with the facts will serve to build a base of support that is so important to success at the building level. Don't worry if you can't do everything that your advisory groups want you to do; just be prepared to act when you can and have good reasons for why you can't comply with "reasonable" requests.

Recommendation 8: Brainstorm With Trusted Colleagues to Find Solutions to Hypothetical Situations That Call for Difficult Decisions

Brainstorming with colleagues can help you not only identify opportunities and avoid pitfalls but also recognize that each situation has its own set of factors that must be considered. This exercise will also demonstrate that there is no one generalization that holds for all people in all situations. Educators must have contingency plans and use their artistry in implementing them.

Recognize that educational leadership is filled with unanticipated consequences. You live in a world where everyone wants a "piece of the action" at every step of the way. It is impossible to create hypothetical responses to every possible scenario, but draw on past experiences to forecast possibilities in the present.

Recommendation 9: As Superintendent, Create a "Supercommittee" of Advisors

If you are a superintendent, create and manage a "supercommittee" consisting of high-level leaders, including corporate giants in the community. This will give you an opportunity to discuss important issues with others who understand high-level decision making. Your community of support will be noticed, increasing your credibility in the district. If you are a subordinate to the superintendent, observe carefully what the superintendent does or does not do with regard to this recommendation, and make plans for how you would treat this matter if and when you are in a position to do so.

In many communities, the position of superintendent of schools is still a highly prestigious position and certainly one of high visibility. Affiliation with a supercommittee will cause your many stakeholders, including the board of education, to begin to recognize you as the chief executive officer of education in your community. Due to the "company that you keep," you will be able to make the necessary contacts that will make your very difficult job somewhat easier to do.

Recommendation 10: Recognize That Both You and Your Organization Can Make Mistakes That Can Lead to Derailment

We refer to the mistakes you make that lead to derailment as the *personal face of derailment* and the mistakes an organization makes as the *organizational face of derailment* (Lombardo & Eichinger, 1995). We have mentioned this several times, but the following list of formal or de facto developmental processes and beliefs of organizations will make clear how cognitive fallacies held by such organizations can lead to derailment:

1. Giving more attention to educational experience and job rotations than to aspiring subordinates

2. Moving people so quickly that they simply don't have time to complete a job successfully (for many leaders, this means that their mistakes don't catch up with them)

3. Moving people laterally from one low-challenging job to another so that they don't learn from new experiences

4. Knocking an educational leader off track for one mistake, whereas successful leaders openly admit that their risk taking has naturally led to mistakes from which they have learned

5. Appointing too many so-called sharks to the fast track, where their aggressiveness, arrogance, and autonomous styles begin as strengths but end as liabilities

6. Giving too much attention during feedback sessions to *what you did,* with little attention given to *how you did it*

7. Defining challenges as moving up the ladder when, in fact, one can often find greater challenges in moving toward learning situations, wherever they may occur

8. Confusing traditional signs of intelligence with common-sense learning acquired through a variety of experiences. (Lombardo & Eichinger, 1995)

Awareness of the cognitive fallacies listed above can help you realize that derailment, in the event that it becomes a part of your career path, isn't necessarily your fault. Once again, you don't have to pay interest on a debt you don't owe.

Recommendation 11:
Don't Forget to Be True to Yourself

Being true to yourself is ultimately the only benchmark of any significance. We live in an outcome-based society where standards of success for educators, particularly superintendents, are higher test scores, more high school graduates attending prestigious universities, and so on. But those measures are secondary to your internal compass of success (Brubaker & Coble, 2005).

Try analyzing your basic assumptions about what really matters and then honing those premises into educational purpose. Ask yourself, "How has my leadership contributed to this purpose?"

CONCLUSION

The main thing to take from this chapter is this: Your intentionality or desire to avoid derailment is an important first step and, when grafted to useful knowledge, can be most effective in both avoiding and dealing with derailment.

We now turn to the important role personal and organizational plans for improvement can play in helping educational leaders both avoid and deal productively with derailment.

CHAPTER FIVE

Professional and Personal Plans for Development

By most accounts, the brand of inservice training we have been offering teachers and administrators has not proven to be effective for helping them gain the deep content knowledge, classroom management and interpersonal skills, technological know-how, understanding of schools as organizations and other concepts and attitudes required by an increasingly complex educational context.

—Betty Fry (in Collins, 2000, p. ix)

W e are convinced that professional development for school and school-system administrators is the key in preventing and dealing with derailment. Derailment leads to an incredible amount of waste in human resources, which causes a heavy personal and organizational toll.

If you pick up almost any article or book on curriculum or instructional leadership, you will discover the following two common findings: (1) the formally appointed leader of the organization, such as the principal or superintendent, sets the tone for all within the organization; and (2) professional development is a major vehicle the formally appointed leader can and should use as a teacher educator, as an administrator educator, or as both.

It is important in giving leadership to professional development for prospective and current educational administrators to recognize the primary role that school and school-system administrators play in the professional development process. Most educators we talk to tend to locate professional development leadership in schools of education at universities. This is probably in large measure due to the fact that, in most parts of the United States, universities control administrator credentialing by teaching courses that lead to the assignment of credentials by state departments of education. Because of this, professors of education consider themselves, and are considered by school leaders, to be teacher and administrator educators. But, in fact, much if not most of this responsibility is in the hands of school and school-system leaders. For example, the day-to-day supervision of master's, sixth-year, and doctoral interns in administration is done by assistant principals, principals, and central office leaders. School and school-system administrators serve as models for interns. Interns want to be assistant principals, not professors of education, and they know that their employment opportunities depend primarily in finding advocates in schools and school systems rather than at the university.

In short, we strongly believe that school and school-system leaders will be the main players in giving leadership to administrator education programs centering on the derailment problem. This is not to minimize the supportive role that professors of educational leadership can play in working with schools and school systems; it is to say, however, that it is essential we be direct and honest about who will hold primary responsibility for helping educational leaders avoid and deal with derailment issues.

WHAT WORKS AND DOESN'T WORK
IN PROFESSIONAL DEVELOPMENT

We begin this chapter with a discussion of what we feel works and doesn't work for educational leaders who are participants in professional development. This discussion will set the stage for the remainder of the chapter, which is devoted to helping you, the reader, create a personal development plan for improvement. In using the ideas in this chapter, we have discovered that they are especially helpful to two groups of educators: those of you who are heading for an assistant principalship, for whom the whole universe of derailment possibilities is relatively new, and those of you already in assistant principalships, principalships, and central office leadership positions, for whom the more subtle causes of derailment are of special significance.

Step 1

The first step in giving leadership to administrative professional development aimed at preventing derailment is to *identify the one overarching characteristic you want a child you love to have when he or she graduates from high school.* Once you have engaged yourself in this exercise, you can involve colleagues in professional development activities to also participate in what we have found to be the most absorbing of professional development challenges. (The careful wording of this initial step is the key to provoking discussion. The phrase *one overarching characteristic* obliges participants to make a forced-choice decision.)

Seymour Sarason (1995), emeritus Professor of Psychology at Yale University, has both framed and answered this question in his seminal work, *Parental Involvement and the Political Principle:* "If when a child is graduated from high school that child is motivated to learn more about self and the world, then I would say that schooling has achieved its overarching purpose" (p. 135). The awe, wonder, and amazement that a child has as a beginning student should be nurtured by the schooling process (Brubaker, 2004). Sarason (1995) adds, "To want to continue to explore, to find answers to personally meaningful questions, issues, and possibilities is the most important purpose of schooling" (p. 136). It is interesting to note how Sarason's question about overarching purpose acquired personal meaning when framed in terms like *"a child I love."*

How is this overarching purpose-of-schooling statement helpful to professional development leaders involved in preventing and dealing with derailment? Overarching purpose can serve as a beacon, much like a lighthouse: It can give us a sense of direction. It can also help us assess present practices to see if they are consistent with our rhetoric about overarching purpose. If such consistency exists, chances of derailment are minimized and the educational leader has the self-assured sense of authenticity from "walking the talk" and being centered.

Step 2

Sarason's (1995) comments point us to the second step in providing professional development opportunities for administrators interested in preventing and dealing with derailment: These opportunities must help administrators associate personal meaning with them. School and school-system administrators tell us that many of their professional development programs are designed to introduce them to recent fads that they are expected to implement in much the same way that a technician installs new hardware. A principal expressed this best: "It's like being ordered to move sandbags from Point A to Point B, and then back again. It is little more than meaningless activity." Real change is "the opposite of a fad or fashion" (Sarason, 1996, p. 91). A convergence of forces produces something new and personally meaningful to participants. We may say, when this happens, that those involved in real change achieve a new understanding of self and act in a way that is consistent with this knowledge (Sarason, 1996).

This understanding of self is sometimes found in places you wouldn't expect it to be found. A relatively new high school principal describes the joy of this discovery:

> I'm thunderstruck at the job that faces me as a high school principal on those rare occasions when I have time to think. I plunged into this job two years ago and am just coming up for air. Regional conferences are the only chance for reflection. Now, my doctoral program gives me a chance to plan to think again.

Step 3

A third step is that educational administrators interested in derailment must involve those they expect to influence in the planning, implementation, and evaluation of professional development activities so that ownership for such activities is assured. If representatives from the larger group of participants are involved in planning, they will become a core group that shares their enthusiasm for professional development activities that follow. In the process, they will help professional development leaders sharpen their efforts.

Step 4

A fourth step is recognizing that much, perhaps most, of the learning from professional development efforts on derailment will occur in informal rather than formal settings. When participants are truly motivated by professional development activities, they share their new knowledge with each other during breaks, after sessions, and before the next day's work. It is sometimes said that we are what we eat, but it is also true that we are what we talk about.

Step 5

The fifth and final step in giving leadership to administrative professional development is recognition by you, the leader, that the more you are involved in learning or the more curious you are, then the more likely it is that others will be involved in learning. A professional development leader said it this way, with a twinkle in his eye:

I think that at least one person here today should have a really good time and learn a lot and I would like to nominate myself. If I am really turned on to learning, it is more likely that you will also be turned on to learning.

To have this spirit is to have all of the feelings associated with risk taking, for you will no longer be the so-called answer person—the kind of leader who views participants as empty vessels to be filled. Patrick Welsh (1987), author of *Tales Out of School*, describes this risk-taking feeling: "The books on pedagogy stress the importance of control in the classroom. But it's when things get a little out of control that real learning takes place" (p. 16).

Implementation Vehicles

Now that we have identified steps involved in implementing staff development activities aimed at preventing and dealing with derailment, we must address another important question: *What vehicles can I use to implement my basic assumptions about staff development for school and school-system administrators?* The following outline may be useful in answering this question:

1. *Cases* demonstrating how school and school-system administrators have avoided and dealt with derailment can be useful. Simply stated, the case approach is the next best thing to being there (Stake, 1995). Lee Shulman (1995) argues that "cases serve as a bridge between theory and practice." Dan Lortie (1995) adds, "Uncertainty is a built-in feature of good cases and perfect solutions do not often arise in their analysis. We acknowledge rather than deny the 'messy' nature of administrative work" (p. 6). (See the Resources section at the end of this book for cases dealing with derailment of educational leaders.)

2. *Seminars and workshops* can be effective vehicles for presenting and discussing ideas on derailment. The key is to have activities that actively involve participants.

3. *Regularly scheduled meetings of administrators* can involve more than the sharing of technical information. Cases can be used to quickly introduce examples of derailment after which discussion can be invited.

4. *Formative and summative evaluation of school and school-system leaders* can be an excellent opportunity to share

ideas related to derailment. The main advantage of this vehicle is that it often takes place in a one-on-one situation, during which an honest sharing of ideas may occur. The degree of stress experienced by not only the person being evaluated but also the evaluator will depend on the history of their relationship and their track records. Summative evaluations are usually more stressful than formative ones.

5. *Mentoring* can be a nurturing vehicle that also provides the power of example for the relatively new member of the school system. The effective mentor conveys the feeling that "I care about you and your professional and personal growth." The key, rather obviously, is who is paired with whom. When the mentoring relationship is right, ideas about derailment can be shared in an honest and forthright way.

6. *Providing opportunities for others to lead* can be a rewarding activity that gives potential leaders an opportunity to try out their wings. The confidence and learning gained from such experience can be instrumental in helping new educational leaders avoid derailment.

7. *Commitment to action programs and taking both potential and present leaders backstage in the process* can provide them with knowledge not found in textbooks. Those taken backstage will also feel trusted with important information as to how to avoid derailment.

8. *Stories and narratives about successful leadership* are ways to communicate what should and can be done to avoid and deal with derailment. The choice of stories is less significant than what they symbolize to the narrator and the listener.

9. *Study groups* can be used to discuss derailment. A small group of elementary school principals met monthly in early morning sessions at different schools to discuss matters related to derailment.

10. *Retreats* can involve administrators in get-togethers away from school sites where they won't be constantly interrupted by the everyday demands of their jobs. We sometimes call these *advances,* which adds an interesting and humorous twist to planning for such events.

PROFESSIONAL DEVELOPMENT RECOMMENDATIONS FOR A SCHOOL OR SCHOOL SYSTEM

Thus far in this chapter, we have discussed the role that professional development can play with regard to the derailment issue. We now move to a list of recommendations that your school system may well find useful in helping leaders both avoid and deal effectively with derailment.

Recommendation 1: Help Others Recognize and Refine Their Talents

Recognize that your challenge is to help leaders identify, use, and refine talents that they may or may not recognize in themselves. We have found the talent inventory shown in Table 5.1 helpful in meeting this challenge. The participant who completes this inventory will be fleshing out a portrait of his or her calling or vocation.

During a typical day at work, you will use more talents than you probably realize you have. Your first task in this inventory is to write, in the first (left) column, a chronology of an ideal (best) day in the school year. Please do this from the time you get up in the morning until the time you go to sleep at night. The first item or two may read something like this: "6 A.M. got up; 6:15 A.M. showered and put on favorite clothes; 6:30 A.M. ate a good breakfast," and so on.

In the second column, list the unique qualities or talents you used, corresponding with the times you listed in the first column. Each of these qualities is a "tape" that goes off in your head when you encounter a particular situation. For example, "at

8:15 A.M., I used my organizational and communication skills to answer students' questions in the office."

In the third column of the inventory, name the sources of the tape you listed in the second column. These sources may include a parent or parents, a teacher, a religious figure, an aunt or uncle, a grandparent, a friend, or others. For example, "at 9 A.M., I took the students to the media center and introduced them to basic computer skills for finding materials. My aunt, an alumna of the college I attended, introduced me to its library. I've loved libraries and media centers ever since."

In the final column, write your decision either to keep and act out the tape from childhood, or reverse the tape and not act it out as you were instructed to as a child. For example, "at 2 P.M., I used my intelligence and physical bearing to break up a fight at school. The tape that went off in my head was to get away from the fight. That's what my parents, teachers, and other adults taught me. But then I reversed the tape, because I knew that in my role as assistant principal, I had to address the matter rather than walk away from it."

The purpose statement at the end of the inventory should be used to summarize what happens when you use your unique qualities or talents as an educational leader.

Table 5.1   A Talent Inventory

Chronology of an Ideal (Best) School-Year Day	My Unique Qualities or Talents Used at This Time of Day (Tapes)	Sources of These Tapes	Personal Decisions to Keep These Tapes or Reverse Them

Purpose Statement: My purpose is to use my talents of _____, _____, and _____ to support and inspire others to identify and use their talents.

Hundreds of educators have responded to this talent inventory. Some of the talents they have listed are preparation skills; proactivity; follow-through; the ability to articulate, verbally and in writing; a sense of humor; the ability to motivate others to work together on committees; being a good team member; and being firm but fair with students (Brubaker, 2004). In reading this list of talents, it is interesting to note that they are precisely the qualities missing in administrators who derailed. (See Chapter 3, "What Causes Educational Leaders to Derail?")

Recommendation 2: Give Educational Leaders Challenges and Get Them Involved

Talents are discovered and self-esteem is gained when educational leaders are placed in challenging situations from which they can learn. Educational leaders we have surveyed and interviewed tell us that, at the beginning of their careers, they felt a tug-of-war take place within them between two forces: "get involved" versus "stay back." Yet they agree, to a person, that they learned only from being involved.

One of the most interesting and satisfying experiences a staff development leader can have is to watch a neophyte leader become a seasoned leader who learns to deal with uncertainty in a self-assured way. The leader who learns from experience has enough of an edge to be involved, but not so much that others lose confidence in him or her.

Experience also teaches the educational leader the importance of knowing what he or she doesn't know and then deciding what to do about this void. It is the challenge of learning new and useful things that motivates the unfinished leader.

A school-system's or school's seasoned leaders are in a unique position to find challenging situations where teacher leaders and beginning administrators can try out their wings while still having a safety net of support from those who care about them.

Recommendation 3: Provide Feedback

Educational leaders need honest and helpful feedback on their progress. The major complaint we have heard about evaluation and feedback is that participants largely get either negative or positive feedback. That is, there is a lack of balance in the assessment process. We can't always expect positive feedback, but when we are criticized, it can be done in such a way that the evaluator conveys confidence that we can improve and feel better for having done so. The person who gives us only praise probably wants our approval at all costs. The person who gives us only criticism is usually projecting his or her own insecurities on us. Neither extreme is helpful to our growth and development.

The artistry of the person giving feedback is evident when the person being assessed asks for advice on how to improve one area or another. This is a sure indication that both assessor and subject have bought into the development process for the good of the organization and the person.

This artistry was brought home to us by a doctoral student and principal, who said this:

> I just finished an evaluation of a difficult teacher. I was originally going to categorize her—give her a number (1, 2, or 3) and move on. Instead, I decided to ask her a question (reframe the evaluation format). "I hear what you're saying (your stated theory) about the music program. How does that match up with what you're doing in class?" We had great dialogue. I, the principal, learned a lot, and her comments suggested that she did too.

Recommendation 4: Recognize That Professional Development Is a Group Activity

All educational leaders should participate in the professional development system. A main advantage of this is that a group of educational leaders, usually at the beginning stage of their career, don't feel that they are pawns being *done unto,* but instead sense that they are included or being *done with.* Experienced leaders who demonstrate that they can take criticism and change set a powerful example for others.

Any organization has contradictions that demand hard work to be reconciled. When there is too great a distance between what the organization says it values and what it really values in its actions, there is bound to be a morale problem. For example, the superintendent who accepts a large raise when teachers and others receive no raise or a minimal one will have his or her credibility eroded. Or the principal who talks about shared decision making but then dumps responsibilities on assistant principals and teacher leaders also becomes a walking contradiction. (See the Resources section at the end of this book for exercises on contradictions.)

Recommendation 5: Be Willing to Make Changes to the Development Program

No professional development system is perfect. Make it clear to all concerned that your system is open to suggestions for improvement. Too often, we introduce a new system as a carefully wrapped package, a perfect product that must not be tampered with in any way. This is an easy trap to fall into, because those who create the system have invested a good deal of time and effort. Those who construct the system must keep their egos in check and value what can be accomplished more than they value being personally rewarded for their input. The *effectiveness* of a system, something that invites alteration and error, must be more important than the *efficiency* of the system.

A PERSONAL DEVELOPMENT PLAN FOR IMPROVEMENT

Effective leaders have a sense of destiny and see their legacy in those they lead (Peck, 1993). A personal development plan must, therefore, begin with the question, "What is my sense of calling?" We commonly think of vocation as one's job or career, but the Latin verb *vocare*, "to call," has a much deeper and more comprehensive meaning.

Think for a moment about what your sense of calling was when you first became a teacher. Many leaders we interviewed talked about their love for children and desire to meet their needs.

You may wish to return to the Talent Inventory (Table 5.1) in the previous section of this chapter to get in touch with your sense of calling and the persons who fueled it. Most people who have completed the Talent Inventory identify important people in their lives who saw talents they often didn't recognize in themselves. (See Case 1, "Getting on Track," in the Resources section at the end of this book.)

You are now faced with the question, "How does my present position fit with my sense of calling?" If there is a fit, you are on course with your self-development plan. If not, what options are open to you to follow? For example, one assistant high school principal discovered that her definition of her role was the key to being aligned with her sense of calling: "When I became an assistant high school principal, I didn't know what I was doing; I thought I was the instrument of punishment. I've learned to be the instrument of positive behavioral change." Another high school assistant principal found that he had to move into the role of principal to get on track with his sense of calling, due to the way his former principal had defined his role as assistant principal:

> When I was an assistant high school principal, the principal measured my success by the number of kids I disciplined. The tone for the school was set by the principal, who seemed to always be looking for students to do something wrong. The school appeared to be run for the convenience of the staff rather than what was good for the students. When I got my own school, I could set the tone in a more positive way.

Now that you have given attention to your sense of calling and your talents, those gifts you have given to others and yourself, we ask you to revisit Chapter 2, "Self-Assessment Checklists," and Chapter 3, "What Causes Educational Leaders to Derail?" Please list the strengths and weaknesses/challenges of your present leadership style. A sample list of an educational leader's strengths and weaknesses follows:

Strengths	*Weaknesses/Challenges*
Proactive, energetic, bright	Impatient; sometimes take on too many tasks at once
Compassionate, warm, personable	Need to listen better
Excellent problem solver	Inclined to micromanage
Excellent follow-through	Need to delegate and trust team members more
Curious, love learning and improving	Sometimes tell people more than they want to hear and come across as expert on everything
Can make tough decisions	Sometimes make snap judgments

Next, we invite you to assess the degree of satisfaction you have in your present position in light of the strengths and weaknesses/challenges you have identified:

1. _____

2. _____

3. _____

4. _____

We would now like to have you identify one or more weaknesses/challenges that you can work on to improve your job performance and to experience more satisfaction in your present position:

Weaknesses/Challenges on Which I Can Work

1. _____

2. _____

3. _____

Your challenge at this point is to find ways to move from where you are in your present position to where you want to be in this position. Please reread the previous section of this chapter with an eye on activities and advice that can help you lead better and achieve more satisfaction in your present position. List those activities and words of advice that may be helpful in your action plan:

Activities and Advice

1. _____

2. _____

3. _____

4. _____

5. _____

It is often helpful to have a colleague or trusted friend play the role of adviser or mentor. Ask this person to add to your list of activities and advice and discuss with this person ways in which your involvement in such activities will help you reach your goal of improved job performance and satisfaction.

Activities	*Ways in Which Activities Can Help Me Reach Goals*
1. _____	_____
2. _____	_____
3. _____	_____
4. _____	_____
5. _____	_____

It should be clear up to this point that *you*, along with the help of your mentor, have decided what changes should be made, how they should be made, and at what time they should be made. In short, this is *your* development plan for improving your leadership in your present position.

Although it is not pleasant to anticipate difficulties during a honeymoon, the time when you are constructing plans for a better future, it can be useful to identify possible barriers or pitfalls that may face you when you begin to implement your self-development plan. We ask you to list these now:

Possible Barriers

1. _____

2. _____

3. _____

4. _____

5. _____

It can be helpful to discuss these barriers with your mentor, who may anticipate barriers you have overlooked. Your mentor may also advise you how to deal with barriers on your list.

Barriers	*Advice*
1. _____	_____
2. _____	_____
3. _____	_____
4. _____	_____
5. _____	_____

It now remains for you to do the hard work of implementing your plan of action for making improvements in your leadership. It is the doing of this work in tough situations that will make you an effective leader. You may return to the preceding lists to check your progress and keep you on course.

Most of you are probably considering other educational positions within or outside of your present school system. The exercises designed to improve your leadership in your present situation may be revisited for positions you are considering. You will, in the process, make an educated guess as to future job satisfaction and fit. It must be added that creative leaders always negotiate the matter of fit.

Dynamics of Development

The Center for Creative Leadership (1995) in Greensboro, North Carolina, has identified the following important questions related to the dynamics of development:

- What strengths do I have that may eventually become weaknesses? (e.g., high decisiveness may lead to arrogance)
- Do I have certain skills that I rely on too much in certain situations? What are those skills? When do I tend to overuse them?
- Which of my skills aren't as sophisticated as they need to be in the future? (e.g., "All my team-building skills have been developed in stable situations")
- Which skills may not matter as much in the future as they do now? (e.g., "My technical skills won't be as important")
- What new skills might be required of me in the next 12 months? (e.g., "I'll have to deal with conflict and ambiguity as we reorganize our structure")
- What flaw do I have that hasn't been a problem before, but that may suddenly matter? (e.g., "I'm creative and lack attention to detail. This now matters because ...") (p. 12)

The dynamics of development are so important and interesting that we invite you to both revise and add to the list of questions just cited. Your answers to these questions will be guiding principles for your leadership efforts.

CONCLUSION

Professional development, the development of persons and schools or school systems, is really all about learning—the learning of persons and schools or school systems. Nancy Dixon (1995) speaks eloquently about this relationship. She reminds us that learning is much more than the acquisition of knowledge already known, that learning is a verb connoting action rather than a noun, and that part of this action is finding meaning, which becomes part of our newly constructed knowledge base. This is certainly a thesis consistent with the philosophical position known as *constructivism.*

We must continue to explore ways in which persons can rethink and create effective, not simply efficient, learning settings that, in turn, respect the creative talents of persons. Much of this challenge will be worked out with the talent pool of future school and school-system leaders. It is this challenge that is the subject of the next chapter, "Preparing Teacher Leaders for Tomorrow's Leadership Positions."

CHAPTER SIX

Preparing Teacher Leaders for Tomorrow's Leadership Positions

The next generation of the teacher-as-leader debate must break new ground; schools must be conceptualized around leadership frameworks that promote a rethinking of teachers' work.

—N. Cranston (2000, p. 123)

The great teachers fill you up with hope and shower you with a thousand reasons to embrace all aspects of life.

—P. Conroy (2002, p. 63)

This chapter is written for teacher leaders and those who give leadership to teacher leaders: assistant principals, principals, and central office leaders, including superintendents.

Much of the information will be new to teacher leaders. Others can use the chapter as a kind of checklist to see how they are doing in their present positions. The connection between this chapter and derailment will be obvious: Information learned and applied can prevent derailment and help you stay on track, and, if derailment occurs, help you, the reader, deal with it.

Tomorrow's educational leaders have an important advantage that many of today's educational leaders didn't have: They are teachers in schools and school systems that have afforded them opportunities to practice leading before assuming assistant principalships, principalships, and central office positions. Recent efforts to flatten organizations and involve teachers more in school governance have given teacher leaders the chance to see if they want to be school administrators and, if so, the kind of school leaders they wish to be as they try to make a difference in the lives of children and adults. In short, we have created *within* school systems and schools an administrator preparation system potentially much more powerful than similar efforts at colleges and universities. Many teachers have experienced leadership over a sustained period of time rather than simply reading about it in textbooks and participating in a brief internship.

This relatively recent phenomenon has its roots in educational reform legislation and implementation, which demand that teachers assume leadership roles. Teachers need leadership skills to motivate students and colleagues, communicate with and influence parents, identify and use human and nonhuman resources, and deal effectively with education issues and challenges. We are moving toward a level of decentralization in some school systems wherein schools take on responsibilities formerly residing in central offices: professional development, textbook selection, use of the school day, decisions regarding innovative instructional programs, and a whole range of administrative decisions, such as the scheduling of students and teachers and budgets.

Derailment is an organizing theme that can be of real value to university and school-system leaders as they provide professional development opportunities for teacher leaders who will be tomorrow's assistant principals, principals, and central office leaders. Subthemes are (a) how to prevent derailment and (b) how to deal with it effectively when it occurs.

A GROUNDING FOR TEACHER LEADER DEVELOPMENT

Initially, we must recognize that those who are interested in teacher leader development have a set of beliefs or commitments that serve as a foundation or grounding for more technical strategies and tactics. Therefore, we wish to identify and discuss the basic beliefs that we hold with regard to teacher leader development. These basic beliefs or groundings are often silent assumptions that contribute to our success or lack thereof in solving problems and reconciling dilemmas.

Six Commitments to Teacher Leader Development

Commitment 1. Schools and schooling must be grounded in democratic principles. It is both desirable and possible to realize this commitment. Engle and Ochoa (1988) spell out some of these principles:

- The most basic value of democracy is respect for the dignity of the individual.
- Individuals and groups have a right to participate in decisions within the society as a whole.
- All citizens have a right to be informed.
- Democracy assumes an open society in the sense that it is never completed. There are no final solutions, no unquestioned answers.
- Democracy assumes some independence of the individual from the group. An open society requires that individuals achieve some autonomy from their own group. (pp. 9–10)

Our first and central belief is that democratic principles must be at the core of our schools and school systems. All following commitments build on this basic belief.

Commitment 2. We strongly support the commitment that a teacher leader development program must give attention to both political power and spiritual power. As M. Scott Peck (1993) has stated so eloquently, "Political power is a matter of externals and spiritual power a matter of what is within" (p. 128). If our teacher leaders focus only on the political, they will pay a high price when they become principals and central office leaders. Hedrick Smith (1988) describes this price: "Politicians strike me as a lonely crowd, making few deep friendships because almost every relationship is tainted by the calculus of power: How will this help me?" (p. 92). Recall that one of the major causes of leader derailment is the self-serving school or school-system administrator who leaves others with the impression that his or her personal advancement is the only thing that matters. The teacher or school administrator who is strictly political locates power outside of self. Gloria Steinem (1992) describes this matter: "Hierarchies try to convince us that all power and well-being come from the outside, that our self esteem depends on obedience and measuring up to their requirements" (pp. 33–34).

The political orientation described above is realized in a top-down governance style, a bureaucratic model for governance: In such an organization, leaders (a) anticipate public reaction, (b) make the decision, and (c) implement the decision (Brubaker, 2005). Once again, this leadership style is reactive and locates power in public reaction to the exclusion of what the leader's internal moral compass has to say. Sociologist Max Weber described this best:

> [Bureaucracy by] its special nature develops the more perfectly the more bureaucracy is "dehumanized," the more completely it succeeds in eliminating from official business love, hatred, and purely personal, irrational, and emotional elements which escape calculation. This is the specific nature of bureaucracy. (quoted in Gerth & Mills, 1964, pp. 215–216)

Rollo May (1975) asks, "What price do we pay for this dehumanization?" and answers, "We deny ourselves the opportunity to directly encounter other persons. Instead of participating in the creative process, "we worship technique . . . as a way of evading the anxiety of the direct encounter" (p. 101).

If we entertain the creativity within us, we risk the anxiety of the direct encounter. We are not afraid to be proactive. When we release our creative and spiritual selves, we find the higher ground that helps us reconcile the many contradictions facing us as school and school-system leaders. We then ask the following hard questions that make us much more than technicians seeking quick fixes:

1. Our school's children are getting higher test scores, which pleases the parents and the board of education, but are they really learning more or learning what is important to learn?

2. They talk about teamwork in this school and school system, but the most prestigious honor is a solitary one—Teacher of the Year. What can we do to make our actions more consistent with our rhetoric?

3. Board members talk about hiring the best people for jobs but pressure us to nominate their own favorites for positions. What can we do about this inconsistency?

Commitment 3. Collaborative decisions are not necessarily better than noncollaborative ones. Bonnie and Clyde, notorious bank robbers, certainly collaborated, but to what end? A friend told us that he was teaching a science lesson in seventh grade, and a student brought a muskrat into the classroom. The question was raised, "Is this muskrat male or female?" A student suggested that students vote to decide whether the animal was male or female. Collaboration in this case could simply lead to a sharing of ignorance.

Collaboration has many advantages, such as getting persons involved in owning the decision-making process as well as the decisions made, but it does not assure that a particular decision is good or morally sound. (See Resource C, "Working Alone and

Working With a Team," in the Resources section at the end of this book.)

Commitment 4. Those involved in professional development efforts for teacher leaders can invite teachers to lead, but it is a serious mistake to force them to do so.

We encountered this matter in a school involved in the shared decision-making process. A new teacher came on board, a teacher who had been actively involved as a team leader in Florida. We were delighted that she had joined our team of teachers in this elementary school. In fact, one of the things that got her the job was her rich experience as a team leader in her previous position in the Florida school. We simply assumed that she would be one of the six team leaders in our shared decision-making project. We said to her, "Judy, we are so glad you are here. We know you will want to be a team leader representing your grade level." She cringed and said, "I burned out in my last school. I was a member of the leadership team, chair of the hospitality committee, and curriculum representative to central office. I want to take some time off from leadership responsibilities to reflect on my teaching." We were, of course, disappointed, but reminded ourselves that she had every right not to be a member of the leadership team. In fact, had we tried to coerce her to take the position, we would have had a less-than-effective leadership team member.

It is also the case that a formally designated committee, such as the school leadership team, will sometimes fail to deliver over the course of a fairly long period of time, after which the principal will turn to another committee to do the job. For example, in one school where we worked, the school leadership committee turned into a "gripe group" because half of its members refused to think positively. They were experiencing difficult home situations that spilled over into their school lives.

The principal could have micromanaged this advisory group by imposing her will on them. Instead, she turned to the social committee as her governance group, and the school climate improved considerably. Once again, forcing a person or group to do what you want them to do simply doesn't work in the long run.

Commitment 5. Attention must be given to communication. Most communication engaged in by school and school-system administrators is verbal rather than written. Listening and speaking are the major vehicles used to communicate.

Part of this process is the construction of a common language. Language is power, as evidenced by the superintendent who always used the term *measurement* when referring to evaluation or assessment. Soon, principals and others in the system spoke only about measurement, thus leaving the impression that student and faculty progress had to have numbers attached to it.

In another school system where we worked, a shared decision-making program was introduced. A teacher in the system asked what we were going to call it. We hadn't given any thought to this matter and quickly said, "The Stone Street Project." Simply naming this in this way evoked a number of unexpected responses by the faculty: "Here we go again; a principal needs a dissertation topic." "Does this mean that we are going to be treated like guinea pigs?" What's in a name? A good deal, we discovered.

One of the most difficult things for teacher leaders to learn is the role of "bracketing" in the communication process. Bracketing is "the temporary giving up or setting aside of one's own prejudices, frames of reference and desires" (Peck, 1978, p. 128). The true listener uses bracketing to temporarily communicate total acceptance of the speaker, the result being that the person speaking will feel less threatened and will make himself or herself more vulnerable by telling you more.

Commitment 6. The learning of all participants in schools and school systems must be at the center of any teacher leader development program. All participants are teachers and learners; they instruct each other in a variety of ways, usually informal, and in turn learn from each other.

Unfortunately, this commitment isn't always voiced in school and school-system public relations pronouncements: "Schools are for children," "Children's learning first." The truth is that adults are very much a part of the transactional teaching-and-learning process along with children.

In addition, adults have to receive at a high level in order to give at a high level (Sarason, 1972). Show us a school or a classroom where adults are learning rather than treating children as empty vessels waiting to be filled, and we will see a school or classroom where children are learning a great deal and, in the process, teaching adult educators something.

One of the difficulties in constructing a framework like the one we have recommended is that it doesn't tell you the degree or kind of commitment a leader is willing to give on a specific issue, such as the desegregation of a school system. Roland Nelson, formerly at the Center for Creative Leadership in Greensboro, North Carolina, has constructed a Commitment Scale/Hierarchy that helps leaders honestly assess what they are willing to do on behalf of a particular commitment to an issue:

1. I will sacrifice my life and/or the lives of my family and/or those I dearly love.

2. I will give up the respect of those whom I love and I'll forego my status and professional achievement.

3. I will forego economic security and my career.

4. I will have serious conflicts between what I think should be done and my reluctance to do it. I may alter my work style and give up those techniques that had previously been successful and beneficial and learn new ones.

5. I will have to alter some habits with which I'm quite comfortable, thus making my job somewhat more difficult. I will feel uncomfortable from time to time as I do things in a way that don't seem, based on my past experience and present assumptions, to be best.

6. Past experience indicates that it doesn't make any difference what I do. My choice, therefore, is between Tweedledee and Tweedledum (described in Brubaker, 2004, pp. 106–107).

An associate superintendent of curriculum and instruction described how Nelson's Commitment Scale was useful to her in relating to two superintendents of schools:

> Five years ago, I made a commitment to a teacher leader development program that was difficult to get off the ground due, in large measure, to an authoritarian superintendent with strong roots in our primarily rural school system. Principals valued their autonomy and resented giving up any power to teachers. Both the superintendent and principals were afraid that a teacher development program would create a new group of principals who would challenge traditional power arrangements in the near future.
>
> A new school board, with a majority of members more suburban than rural, was elected. They moved quickly to urge the hiring of more women and persons of color as principals. Three years ago, a new superintendent from a suburban school system was named, and he made a strong commitment to the school board's priorities—including a teacher leader development program that I would head.
>
> Throughout this change of the school system from rural to suburban and a different emerging kind of school and school-system leadership, I placed the rhetoric and actions of key leaders on the Commitment Scale. I did the same thing with my rhetoric and actions. I found it especially helpful to see discrepancies between what people said they were committed to and what they actually did.

The six commitments we hold with regard to teacher leader development are part of the foundation for the remainder of this chapter. We believe that they are essential in helping teacher leaders learn about how to both prevent and deal with derailment in their own careers as well as in the careers of those they lead. In the next section of this chapter, we give attention to the school context in which teacher leaders develop.

THE REALITIES OF THE CONTEXT
IN WHICH TEACHERS LEAD

It is relatively easy to talk about teacher leadership as an idea, construct, or abstraction that should be introduced and sustained in
schools. It is when teacher leadership is considered *in a particular
context* that reality sets in, because the specific variables facing
teacher leaders come into play. It is these variables that we will discuss in this section of the chapter. It makes sense that most of
these variables deal with the relationship between teacher leaders
and principals.

*The principal is officially responsible for what happens in the
school.* We can talk all we want about flattening the organization,
shared decision making, and the like as desirable alternatives to
top-down traditional management systems, yet we can't eliminate
the fact that one person is officially appointed to accept ultimate
responsibility for what goes on in the school as a whole. That
person is the principal. The buck stops there. If a school goes off
track, the principal is blamed by central office leaders, including
the superintendent.

The superintendent of schools sets the tone for principals and
their schools. If the superintendent not only talks about decentralization and shared decision making but also lives this philosophy
of education, it is more likely the principals will do likewise for
educators in their schools. All will depend on the principal's primary leadership style and his or her willingness to share power.
In short, teacher leadership depends upon the principal, and the
leadership of principals depends upon the superintendent.

One of the biggest difficulties we have had with shared leadership in schools occurs when a principal fails to acknowledge that
leadership councils are, in reality, advisory bodies to the principal.
These representative groups may use a variety of sources of
power, such as expertise, charisma, and succorance, but they do
not have the positional authority delegated to the principal of the
school.

If a principal leaves teacher leaders with the impression
that they have the sort of positional authority assigned to the

principal, these teacher leaders will feel that they have been sold out and that the governance system is a sham when they don't get their way on an important issue.

We witnessed an example of this. The incident occurred in December, a month fraught with difficulties due to the pressures teachers and administrators have at home in the holiday season. Three issues came to a head. The first, and in many ways the most important, issue concerned the location of the teacher assistants' workroom in an elementary school. At the beginning of this shared decision-making project, the assistants were moved from the stage in the cafeteria to an area in the multipurpose room. This area was partitioned by bulletin boards and wasn't the least bit soundproof. Because the physical education teacher and others used the multipurpose room for their activities, it was difficult for assistants to do work that required concentration, and the noise that assistants made working machines disturbed classes held in the multipurpose room. As the cold weather approached, the problem was accentuated, because more physical education classes had to be held inside the school. This raises the question: How can teacher assistants be afforded the dignity and fair treatment given to teachers?

The second issue concerned the supervision of children on the playground during recess time. Some staff members simply weren't supervising students well, with the result being fights and injuries to students. The dilemma may be stated in the form of a question: How can students receive adequate supervision from some teachers and assistants so that other teachers can have time away from the children during recess time?

The cafeteria was the location of the third issue. Once again, some teachers and assistants didn't provide adequate supervision of students. When a cafeteria gets out of hand, the noise level is intolerable, food and other objects are thrown, and pushing, shoving, and fighting occur. The same question could be raised about the cafeteria as was raised about the playground: How can students receive adequate supervision from some teachers and assistants so that other teachers can have time away from children during lunchtime?

The convergence of these three issues within the same time period—the last few weeks prior to vacation for the holidays—is important to keep in mind in our analysis of what happened.

The leadership team, elected by teachers according to grade levels, spent some time discussing these matters, but they were not resolved. One of the team leaders said,

> I knew that things were building up in the principal and something had to be done. I could see the injured children taken into the nurse's room. I also knew that our leadership team was on record as deciding that we didn't have time to discuss the issue until after the holidays.

The result of all of this was a memorandum from the principal that simply stated that (a) teachers would have to accompany their children on the playground during recess time, (b) teachers would have to eat lunch with their children to supervise their behavior, and (c) the assistants would use the teachers' lounge for their workroom, and the teacher's lounge would be relocated in the multipurpose room formerly occupied by assistants. When some teachers asked about the merit of these decisions, the principal assured them that these decisions were clearly within his jurisdiction for he was the officially designated leader of the school.

When teachers returned from the holidays, the principal's holiday ultimatum was very much on their minds. The leadership team and principal discussed the matter at some length. Both sides to the controversy apologized for mistakes made. One thing was clear, however: Teachers and their representative bodies are advisory, and the principal has official responsibility for what goes on in the school.

On occasion, we meet a principal who uses teacher leader advisory groups as scapegoats for what parents and others consider to be bad decisions made by the principal.

Thus far in this section of the chapter, we have focused on the relationship between teacher leaders and their principal. *Consultants often play a key role in shared decision-making governance systems, thereby creating both opportunities and challenges for the teacher leader.* Initially, we must note that there are two kinds of consultants: (a) internal consultants from central office and (b) external consultants from outside of the school system. Perhaps the most important question is this: Did your school initiate contact and ask for the consultant or was the consultant assigned to you? Ideally, one or more leaders in your school identified a need and asked for help in addressing it. However, it is frequently the case that someone in central office assigns a consultant to your school because of a need that *they* perceived to exist.

A director of curriculum and instruction in a fairly large suburban school system takes us backstage on this matter:

> Our superintendent prides himself on his interest in and leadership on behalf of curriculum and instruction. As a result, he and his wife, who works for the state Department of Instruction, make frequent trips to conventions featuring innovative programs and projects. Central office consultants in the various areas of the curriculum, such as math, science, social studies, and language arts, gather the most recent literature on curriculum innovations and send this along with convention advertisements to the superintendent. Sometimes, they deliver it in person to make their sales pitch. And, it works!
>
> Our arts program, for example, had tremendous human and nonhuman resources given to it after our superintendent went to a convention and heard a speech on connoisseurship by Eliot Eisner of Stanford University. Eisner was brought in as a consultant, and we used many of his materials. The arts are usually the first to be cut in this age of accountability and high-stakes testing, and our superintendent's interest in Eisner's work made a very positive difference in our school system.

One of the first questions teacher leaders must address is the relationship between the consultant(s) and the principal. In the case just described, the principal had no previous knowledge of the consultant or his work. The superintendent also had no special relationship with the consultant. In a few instances, the principal or central office leader has a vested interest that complicates matters for teacher leaders.

For example, in one school system, the superintendent needed a dissertation topic and research project to complete his doctorate at a nearby university. The superintendent used the school and staff of a trusted friend, who was a middle school principal, to introduce a shared decision-making project. This questionable practice, which usually involves the hiring of the dissertation adviser or a doctoral dissertation committee member as a consultant, has unfortunately been a norm in many departments of educational administration. The pressure is now on you, the teacher leader, to deliver positive results regarding this so-called experimental project so that the superintendent-cum-doctoral student can complete his degree and declare the project a success, thus building his political capital.

It is helpful to you, a teacher leader, to know what the consultant can and can't deliver. We have encountered the following roles played by consultants with regard to the consultant's expertise:

1. The consultant has the expertise to help the teacher leader in a direct manner. For example, teacher leaders need help in knowing more about decision-making styles and contingency theory, and the consultant has and shares this knowledge.

2. The consultant, although not an expert in the area of concern, acts as a broker to connect teacher leaders with a source of help. For example, the consultant is an expert on organizational governance but is not an expert on a subject that teacher leaders have identified as important: how teachers and staff relate to parents and others in the community. The consultant, therefore, brings in a person who trains airline flight attendants to conduct a staff development program on "presentation of self to the public."

3. The consultant is not an expert in the area of concern, and limited resources keep the consultant from connecting teacher leaders with the expert. For example, the consultant wants to bring in an expert on reaching a group of at-risk students in May, but the consulting budget is exhausted by early April.

4. The consultant isn't an expert in the area of concern and doesn't know any experts who can deal with the issue. For example, a few children in the school appear to be unreachable and act out their frustration in ways that are detrimental to other students. The consultant and teacher leaders are also frustrated but, despite their efforts, they don't know where to turn next.

It is this fourth situation that is obviously most difficult for teacher leaders to face. They and their consultant don't feel they can fix the problem despite their efforts. They are instead left with the understanding that there is a difference between problems that can be solved and dilemmas that must be reconciled.

The challenge to teacher leaders with regard to consultants is to be as proactive as possible in deciding if you need help from outside the school and, if so, to get the kind of help *you want*. Once you set the stage on this matter, the drama seems to have a life of its own. Once a consultant is on board, teacher leaders, the principal, and the consultant should discuss as honestly as possible what kind of relationship you want to have with each other. Teacher leaders should be conscious of the sources of power available to them, such as expertise, charisma, and succorance, so that they can influence the direction the leadership team, the principal, and the consultant take in pursuing their goals.

There is an issue of special importance facing teacher leaders with regard to shared decision-making projects: the dissemination of information, particularly the results of their shared decision-making efforts. Progress reports, news releases, television interviews, and other accounts of events at your school are usually in the hands of administrators and consultants. This model for the dissemination of information is consistent with the bureaucratic model, for those higher up decide (a) if the information should be released; (b) the medium for the release, such as a newsletter, newspaper article, or radio or television appearance; and (c) the manner or tone in which the information is presented. How ironic it is that those closest to the students often have little, if anything, to say about dissemination of information about those children.

We urge teacher leaders to play an active part in giving leadership to the dissemination process. It will give you invaluable experience that will stand you well in the event that you become administrators and it will be satisfying to tell the story as you feel it should be told.

THE TEACHER LEADER AND THE PRESENTATION OF SELF

We noted in Chapter 3 that problems with interpersonal relations were a key factor in an educational leader's derailment. Most of these problems were related to poor skills in the presentation of self. By *presentation of self,* we mean performances—defined as "all the activity of a given participant on a given occasion which serves to influence in any way any of the other participants" (Goffman, 1959, p. 15). The way in which a teacher leader presents himself or herself is a key to personal and organizational success. Effective teacher leaders, like other successful educators, are able to articulate what they are doing and why. This articulation occurs in performances, and these performances take many forms: speaking, written communication (hard copy and electronic), nonverbal communication (body language and fronts), and listening.

The successful teacher leader knows how to use the civilities of leadership, those seemingly small acts that make a positive difference in the culture of the school. When manners and politeness are merged with professional expertise, both the individual—in this case, the teacher leader—and the school profit. We want to demonstrate this by having you complete the following change and conservation inventories:

Inventory 1:   A Personal Change and Conservation Inventory
_____ [My Name]

What are the three things about *my leadership* that I highly value and want to conserve?

1. _____

2. _____

3. _____

What are the three things about *my leadership* that I want to change—that are challenges?

1. _____

2. _____

3. _____

Inventory 2:   Reorganizational Change and Conservation Inventory
_____ [Name of Our School]

What are three things about *our school* that I highly value and want to conserve?

1. _____

2. _____

3. _____

What are three things about *our school* that I want to change—that are challenges?

1. _____

2. _____

3. _____

One of the major values of these inventories is that they recognize that some things have to remain the same for other things to change. Some leaders who talk about changes in a school or school system fail to make this point, thereby leaving others with feelings of instability that they don't necessarily need to have.

As you read the remainder of this section of the chapter on the civilities of leadership, please be mindful of the three following questions:

1. Which of your responses to items in the change and conservation inventories, if any, have to do with the civilities of leadership?

2. After reading this section of the chapter, what civilities of leadership in my leadership style do I want to conserve and change?

3. After reading this section of the chapter, what civilities of leadership in our school do I want to conserve and change?

This exercise may also be used with either large or small groups of persons interested in your school—including students. We have found the inventories to be both provocative and a source of healthy discussion. In some cases, leadership teams administer the inventories with all participants guaranteed anonymity (participants are asked not to sign their names on the Personal Change and Conservation Inventory). In other situations, leadership team members summarize results from their constituents and share these results at leadership team meetings.

Civilities of Leadership

Entrance and Exit Rituals. Entrance and exit rituals are important in any setting where the teacher leader participates. It is useful to remember one of the adages in the luxury hotel business: "If you manage the first and last impressions of a guest properly, then you'll have a happy guest" (Kleinfield, 1989, p. 36). One of the first things hotel workers are told is that eye contact is a necessary behavior for greeting guests when they arrive at the hotel. Such contact communicates your willingness to go out of your way to help people entering the setting, and it says you are risking a certain kind of vulnerability on their behalf. (See Resource B, "Entrance and Exit Rituals," in the Resources section at the end of this book.)

It has been useful to us to observe some leaders as they use smiles and other nonverbal behaviors to relax persons entering a setting. They also frequently exhibit the ability to establish an affinity connection with so-called small talk.

Leaders who have given attention to entrance rituals know the importance of the physical setting. In one school, the leadership council was unhappy with the high counter that served as a barrier between guests and the secretary. Working with the secretary and the principal, the counter was removed to facilitate communication. The same leadership council informed the principal that guests were often greeted in an abrupt manner by one of the receptionists. The principal brought this to the attention of the lead secretary who taught the receptionist to begin conversations with guests by saying something like "Welcome to *our* school. How may I help you?"

A good energy level on the part of the greeter is important, but it is not sufficient in itself. Guests want to know that school leaders have a sense of purpose so that students and adults will be involved in meaningful activity. A clear but concise vision statement communicates this sense of direction: "Everything we do here is aimed at helping students and adults become the best they can be." This general vision statement can be followed by more specific goals for the school.

Teacher leaders and principals can profit from knowing the difference between acceptable *onstage* and *backstage behaviors.* For example, the person who is counting lunch money would do well to do so in the principal's office rather than in the secretaries' area. This responsibility requires uninterrupted concentration. If the person in charge of counting money does so in a public area and considers guests to be an interruption, guests will not feel invited into the school. It is good to remind ourselves that some chaos backstage, for example in the teachers' lounge, is necessary for an orderly environment onstage (Kleinfield, 1989).

Many entrance rituals involve answering questions that guests have about what goes on in the educational setting. Most schools have an open house early in the year. In some cases, parents walk an abbreviated schedule of their child's day at school. I (Brubaker) experienced this a few years ago, with the first class being an algebra class. During the brief question-and-answer period, a mother asked, "Will you tell me if this class will be useful to my son in other math classes and in classes he takes in college?" The algebra teacher responded, "I have no earthly idea." There was a long pause after which the teacher was literally saved by the bell.

My first impulse was to blame the teacher. My second impulse was to blame the principal. My third impulse was to blame teacher educators at universities. I then realized that teachers have probably had little or no instruction during their preservice and inservice education in explaining to parents what they are doing and why. Yet the hallmark of a professional is that he or she can explain what he or she is doing and why. We therefore recommend that the civilities of educational leadership in general, and entrance and exit rituals in particular, be the subject of professional development for teachers, teacher leaders, and administrators.

Exit rituals are also significant. For example, the teacher leader or administrator who walks parents and other guests to the door has the opportunity to prolong their conversation and demonstrate his or her care for the guests. It is an opportunity to summarize what has happened during the visit, thank guests for their interest in the children and the school, and invite them back for another visit. Luxury hotel surveys have also revealed time and again that "guests very much like being called by name" (Kleinfield, 1989, p. 35).

Exit rituals have demonstrated repeatedly that "there is no more loyal guest than one who has a problem that gets fixed" (Kleinfield, 1989, p. 32). Any parent knows not only the anguish felt when his or her child has a problem, but also the joy and relief that comes with the solving of that problem.

We end our discussion of entrance and exit rituals by describing an out-of-town candidate for a teaching position—a person highly recommended to the principal. The night before the interview, the principal received a call from the candidate, complaining about the hotel room assigned. When the principal arrived at the hotel to try to deal with this matter, the candidate had made such a scene in registering the complaint that the desk clerk simply said to the principal, "Please just get this person out of here." At the end of the day of interviews with the principal, teachers, and central office personnel, the candidate simply left town without saying anything to anyone. The principal and others were shocked at the absence of civilities of the candidate. Needless to say, the candidate didn't get the job.

Listening and Speaking. Listening is probably the most powerful civility available to the teacher leader and school administrator. It is flattering to the speaker and demonstrates that you aren't self-centered but instead are eager to learn more about the person speaking. By focusing on the speaker, you will also lessen your anxiety (Linver, 1978). By actively listening, you will communicate that you understand where the speaker is coming from and that you care enough about that person to step into his or her shoes (Linver, 1978).

Speaking is another critical communicative skill that may be important in learning more about yourself and others. How significant is this skill in comparison to writing? Sandy Linver (1978), author of *Speakeasy,* answers this question: "The way we interact with other people—both personally and professionally—has little to do with the written word. It is almost totally based on speaking" (p. 18).

There is no one right speaking style. Rather, a speaker's credibility depends on authenticity or genuineness. It therefore makes sense that the starting place for good speaking is to know what kind of person you basically are.

Please take a moment to complete the following self-inventory. It will give you a start in assessing your comfort and proficiency as a speaker.

Inventory 3: How Good and Comfortable Are You as a Public Speaker?

Please assess your comfort and proficiency on the following items, from 1 (*low*) to 5 (*high*):

Comfort/Proficiency

1. Speaking one on one

2. Listening one on one

3. Answering questions one on one

4. Speaking to a small group

5. Listening (as the speaker/leader) and reading verbal and nonverbal language of the small group

6. Answering questions after speaking to a small group

7. Speaking to a large group

8. Listening (as the speaker/leader) and reading verbal and nonverbal language in a large group

9. Answering questions after speaking to a large group

10. Giving telephone interviews

11. Participating in television interviews at the television station

12. Participating in television interviews on site at the school

13. Giving radio interviews

14. Participating in newspaper reporter interviews

Are you more comfortable relating to people in formal or informal situations? If your style is more informal, push the lectern aside and move into the audience as if you were having a conversation. Once again, draw on your "honesty and courage to be authentic with your audience and project to them who you really are" (Linver, 1978, p. 59). Regardless of your style, the secret is to focus on your audience, rather than yourself, and share your warmth with them. One good way to focus on the audience is to share your sense of humor. This has the effect of relaxing the audience, whether it is one person or 100.

My (Brubaker's) father attended a college alumni meeting in Sarasota, Florida, hundreds of miles away from his alma mater, Albion College, in Michigan. The speaker was the president of the college. My father called me after the speech and raved about the president. "Why did you like him so much?" I asked. Dad responded, "He talked to each of us before the speech about our personal interests in the college and he cared about what we had to say." In short, the president set the stage for his own success before he even spoke a word in the more formal setting. In the process, the president relaxed himself before the speech.

The physical setting in which you speak also sets the stage for your speaking. In both formal and informal settings, it can be useful to have a mental checklist. For example, remove distractions, such as a gurgling coffeepot; have chairs, tables, or other furniture arranged the way you want them; assess acoustics and check equipment; and have a résumé for the person who is introducing you. Your preparation for the situation sends the message, "I care enough about you, the audience, to have done my homework." And good preparation also gives you, the speaker, a sense of security.

You will naturally be nervous to some extent before speaking in many situations. Treat this nervousness as a good thing; it means that you care enough about the audience and yourself to get psyched up for the occasion. Self-talk can be helpful as you prepare: "Good going. I have an edge on and I know that this is necessary to do a good job." It is especially helpful to realize that the audience wants you to succeed and is therefore with you from the start.

One of the advantages speaking has over writing is that you get immediate reaction to your ideas. Because 65% of communication is nonverbal body language (Linver, 1978), you will be able to read your audience and know how your ideas are being received. As you share your warmth with them, they will share their warmth with you.

As teacher leaders and possibly as educational administrators in the future, you will be expected to go on television. We have prepared a list of guidelines for this challenge:

1. Talk to the reporter, not the camera or microphone. Look the reporter straight in the eye.

2. Stand or sit erectly. Don't stoop or bend over.

3. If you say, "No comment," add that you will get back to the reporter by a specific time.

4. Know whom you are dealing with and develop rapport with the reporter when possible.

5. Remember that the good photographer or camera person doesn't necessarily have the camera to his or her eye. The camera can be rolling from any position, even if it is under his or her arm.

6. Be politely on your guard all of the time.

7. Take advantage of nonconfrontational "good news" programs.

8. The bottom line is to meet reporters head-on and be honest. The camera doesn't lie: It will see your eyes.

9. Be cool and confident. It disarms reporters.

10. Remember that there is a high degree of sensitivity about minorities and women at this time in the history of our nation.

11. A smile is the most disarming thing in the world. Bring to the camera the real person inside you.

12. Be prepared. If you don't know, say, "I don't know."

13. There is no such thing as "off the record." Beware of the reporter who says, "This is off the record."

14. You can ask to talk to the reporter about something before you go on camera. If the reporter won't allow you to do this, don't proceed with the interview.

15. It is a good idea to suggest a place for the interview. Get an appropriate backdrop.

16. Watch hazards around you. Don't swivel in a chair. Don't fidget. Calm down, even if it means that you grab a desk in front of you or behind you.

17. Take your time.

18. Ask to reshoot if you are extremely dissatisfied with the interview.

19. Limit the number of remarks and focus on two or three points.

20. Ask the reporter not only who he or she has already talked to, but also who else will be talked to before this story is over.

21. You can occasionally stop a reporter in his or her tracks by saying, "I have no earthly idea what you're talking about."

22. Be alert to the fact that some reporters may subscribe to the "wouldn't you say" school of journalism (Schieffer, 2003, p. 51). A reporter may ask, "Would you say that your school has serious security problems?" If you even nod yes, you may well be quoted as saying, "The principal says his school has serious security problems."

23. The school or central office is private property. Be aware, however, that television cameras can shoot onto your property from a nearby site without your permission.

It should be clear that television is such a volatile medium, one used by more people than any other electronic medium, that it could be a key factor in both preventing and dealing with derailment. Familiarity with television interviews will be enhanced as you have more and more experience with reporters. How does one get better and better at this? Practice, practice, practice. One story has it that Winston Churchill was once asked what he did in his spare time: "He responded, 'I rehearse my extemporaneous speeches'" (Adams, 1983, p. 229).

Writing. Writing affords you another vehicle for communication with parents and others interested in schools. Time and time again, parents share with others messages from educators that have serious spelling and grammatical errors. Teachers' comments on student papers also sometimes have such errors. Parents ask, "How can they teach good writing when they don't know what good writing is?"

Correct spelling and grammar are important civilities of leadership. Because we all make spelling and grammatical errors, the secret is to have a proficient proofreader who will read our memos and other communications. It takes extra effort and time to use a proofreader, but many an embarrassing moment can be avoided by such effort.

An important question to ask in sending an e-mail, letter, or memorandum is, "What is my purpose in doing this?" This purpose should be clearly stated, with concrete next steps spelled out concisely and precisely, so that the parents or other adults know what they are expected to do after reading your communication. In the event that you want to be sure of a reply or to expedite such a response from an individual, ask for it with the original e-mail or include a stamped, self-addressed envelope with a memo or letter.

Finally, always send clean copy. Poorly typed communications and badly photocopied materials send the message that you are sloppy and unprofessional.

Miscellaneous Civilities of Leadership. Other civilities are as follows:

1. When leaving a message on a telephone answering machine or service, state your name, telephone number, the nature of the business, and the best time to return the call. State this information slowly. Remember, the person listening to your request is writing the information down.

2. Before meeting with other persons or having important phone conversations, prepare for the content of the conversation, even if this means writing notes from which you speak.

3. Always give your full name when making a phone call. Many people begin speaking and the other party has no idea who it is.

4. There are two major ways to ensure that you can do something with the support of your so-called bureaucratic superiors: (1) remove irritants and (2) be willing to share the credit if efforts are successful and the blame if they are not.

5. When substantive agreements are arrived at over the telephone, follow up with a memo or e-mail of understanding, concluding with the phrase, "Unless I hear from you otherwise, I'll assume this is correct."

6. Log important contacts with other parties.

We would do well to remind ourselves that all forms of communication are promissory activity (Goffman, 1959, pp. 2–3): We promise that we will act out what we have said we will do. The details of relating to others—what we call the *civilities of leadership*—are an important but insufficient element of creative leadership. When such details are part of the leader's total effectiveness, they have verisimilitude or the ring of truth. The creative leader relates to others and self with honesty, integrity, and authenticity.

THE TEACHER LEADER AND MEETINGS

How may times have you heard educators say that meetings are a waste of time? In the next breath, they expect you to be a productive participant in a meeting where they are the designated leader. They can't have it both ways. The secret is to have meetings when they can be productive and not have them when they are not needed. When a meeting can be productive, it is important to know how to get what you want out of it. In fact, that is the first question the teacher leader must ask: "What is the purpose of the meeting?"

A personal, real-life example from my (Brubaker's) experience will illustrate this matter. We were building the foundation for a new house and I realized that I needed to talk to a few mortgage lending agencies about finances. After each meeting, I returned to my family with a sense of no direction and no accomplishment. In talking with our builder, I learned the exact language necessary to meet my purpose and used it at a meeting with the chief executive officer of a bank after brief small talk concerning how his mother graduated from the university where I was teaching: "What I would like today is preloan approval so that, when the house is built, we will be set to get the mortgage." The CEO looked over the mortgage application and said, "You don't fit the formula, but you can have the preloan approval!" His secretary then typed out a letter to that effect, and our family was on track after several days of not even being at the "station."

Many meetings are like my early meetings with lending institution people. In fact, leaders at such meetings sometimes begin the meeting by saying, "What is it that we need to do today?" A well-run meeting begins by having the assigned leader state the purpose for the meeting. The following is an example of effective teacher leadership in a meeting:

> We have 45 minutes this afternoon for our leadership team meeting. You will note that our agenda is divided into two parts, with information items in Part 2. You can read these on your own. Our purpose for this meeting is to discuss the two items in Part 1: (1) ways in which we can get members of our grade-level teams to give us their views on various subjects more effectively and (2) ways in which we, as members of the leadership team, can communicate more effectively with them. I will take notes on our discussion and send them to you in an e-mail as soon as possible.

Several messages have been sent to committee members with this leader's brief introduction. First, the leader has done her homework by preparing an agenda. Second, the leader doesn't want to waste members' time by going over information items that can be easily read. Third, the leader, because of her experience in previous meetings, has developed a premeeting ritual in which she visualizes what she wants to happen in the meeting, thus giving her confidence from the moment she enters the meeting room, and so she introduces the meeting with a self-assured speaking voice. Fourth, the leader demonstrates that this meeting is important by saying that she will distribute notes from the meeting as soon as possible.

We have attended hundreds of leadership team meetings and can quickly identify those leaders who are real professionals. They are artists who know the correct mix of formality and informality. If the group is moving too much toward one pole or the other, the leader takes steps to achieve proper balance. Committee members leave such meetings with the feeling that much has been done and in an enjoyable way.

One of the biggest challenges facing the teacher leader who is expected to facilitate a leadership team meeting is to keep the tone of the meeting from becoming too negative. A committee will occasionally have a person who simply wants to gripe about everything. Sometimes, such persons are not even conscious of their negative influence. If other members of the committee are engaged in work that leads to positive outcomes, the negative person may well be crowded out of his or her funk. However, at times, the assigned leader will need to directly address the problem in a one-on-one situation.

The teacher leader who is effective in facilitating leadership team meetings actively listens to language used by participants. Language is a kind of emotional shorthand that quickly conveys meanings to people. While sitting in on leadership team meetings, we have collected a number of morale-building and morale-breaking phrases:

Morale-Building Phrases

"I'm relating so much better to _____."

"I can express my ideas in these meetings without being shot down."

"We cooperative despite our differences."

"We go to each other for suggestions because we know that we're accepted."

"No one person dominates in this group."

"When a person in this group takes on an assignment, we know that it will be done."

"When a person from this committee learns something, she brings it back to the group and shares it with all of us."

Morale-Breaking Phrases

"It won't work."

"Too much paperwork."

"It's too late to begin this."

"What's the matter with the way we do it now?"

"The problem is that they are all just too lazy."

"We just don't have the time to do it."

"All those deadlines."

"With this short notice, I don't have any suggestions."

"You'd think someone else would do it."

"They'll never read it anyway."

"I've already got a full load."

"Let's do it some other time."

"It seems to me this is the job of the leader, not us."

"I'm not paid for this."

"Because we don't really make the decision, we're just going through the moves."

We sometimes ask a recorder to write down key emotive terms during a workshop of half a day or so and then have participants tell us what they mean by these terms. The following list illustrates the results of this exercise:

Paperwork—A symbol for waste of time, busywork, extra duties, bureaucratic directives and the bureaucracy itself, and reluctance of the leader to accept responsibility.

Deadline—A symbol for the authority of the leader, the bureaucratic hierarchy, extra duties, and pressure.

Memo or *E-Mail*—A symbol for bureaucratic hierarchy; a well-organized leader who has taken time to remind group members of what has occurred or what will occur; sometimes all are punished for one person's behavior; feeling that some good might have come from the meeting after all.

Activity-Oriented, Hands-On, Manipulative Materials—A symbol for educationese; the need someone feels for students to learn directly by manipulating things.

Objectives, Goals, Rationale—A symbol for boundaries and the need to organize in order to strive toward predetermined outcomes.

Individualized Instruction—A symbol for more work on the teacher's part.

Textbook—A symbol for the "bible"; keeping things as they are (manageable and secure).

Letter or E-Mail From Downtown—A symbol for "God directed" work; more paperwork; the authority and power of bureaucrats.

We to I—A symbol for the leader's move from democratic "we" to "I" in order to draw on higher position of authority as disagreement occurs.

Agreement to Adjourn—A symbol for one thing all support.

Informal Seating Arrangements—A symbol for leader's desire to have cooperative, nonhierarchical sharing of ideas.

Use of First Names—A symbol for cooperation, collegiality, and no hierarchy.

Leader Starts Meeting on Time, Stops When Appropriate, and Has Previously Distributed Agenda—A symbol for the value the leader places on time as a resource for participants.

Leader's Smile and Relaxed But Organized Manner—A symbol for the leader's desire to be there; the acceptance of what group members can do.

Leader's Choice of a Good Meeting Site—A symbol that the leader has done his or her homework and cares about both participants and the meeting.

Leader Squarely Faces Conflict and Differences of Opinion—A symbol for the leader's desire to be honest about his or her own feelings and consciously choosing the best way to express these feelings.

As a leader in meetings, you, the teacher leader, may also wish to participate in this exercise to see what committee members identify as key emotive terms and what they mean.

THE TEACHER LEADER AS NETWORKER

Meetings tend to be somewhat formal in nature, even when a leader is more comfortable with an informal leadership style. Much, if not most, of the teacher leader's effectiveness will depend on his or her networking ability. Networking may be defined as the informal process of actively sharing information and support. Leaders who are comfortable with more autocratic, hierarchical decision-making frameworks usually fear networking, because there are no clear lines of authority and control is not necessarily in the hands of those higher up in the organization.

The electronic revolution in general and the computer revolution in particular are evidence of the growth of networking. Individuals don't have to go through layer after layer of bureaucracies to get what they want. Everything from clothes to cars can be ordered while sitting at your keyboard. The direct participation of constituents without having to go through their elected representatives and the widespread influence of television have created revolutionary changes in our political system. In fact, politicians have to run fast to try to catch up with their constituents.

All of these changes can work to the advantage of teacher leaders as they access and use information. Change can be introduced and maintained, and those things the teacher leader wants to conserve can be safeguarded through effective networking. Shared learning can facilitate a sense of community in a school or a setting within a school.

Networking Suggestions

The following suggestions are the result of observations we have made in watching teacher leaders and other educators use networking as a vehicle for more effective leadership.

Sometimes, just introducing two people to each other will make things happen. A teacher leader related, "I introduced a member of our leadership team to one of my professors at the university who is an expert in reading education. They started sharing resources— ideas and materials—that made their way into our leadership team meetings."

Taking the initiative and acting, not just reacting, can make a difference. A first-year teacher who was asked to join the leadership team shared her feelings about moving from the role of reactor to that of actor: "I was reluctant to contact people at first, but once I got started in building a network, things began to happen and I gained confidence."

Occasionally, drop by for informal conversations with persons in your network. Informal conversations symbolize your personal interest in the lives of people in your network. It is sometimes useful to share materials in order to break the ice. A sense of humor is appreciated.

Give attention to members of other people's support group. It is easy to walk by such persons. While talking to a person in *your* network, listen carefully to discover who the key persons are in his or her support group. A teacher leader describes how this worked for her: "I used to just walk by a particular administrator's secretary, but when I took time to get to know the secretary, I discovered a good deal about this administrator's leadership style. Also, I can get a lot of things done through the secretary that help our leadership team."

Don't always expect immediate results when you introduce change in your network. As a teacher leader, you will sometimes be surprised to find that the seed of an idea planted earlier will surface at a later date. A member of your network will usually forget where he or she got the idea originally and will instead introduce the idea as if he or she originated it.

Don't assume that the chemistry of your one-to-one relationships with persons in your network will be the same when a group of such persons gets together. It is natural to assume that your friends will also be friends of each other, yet we hear of instance after instance of dis-illusionment when network members discover otherwise. "We just thought that our spouses would get along," said one teacher leader, "but the four of us just weren't comfortable when we got together."

Because persons are expected to conform to role expectations in more formal settings, don't be shocked when they act somewhat differently in less formal settings or vice versa. As one teacher leader told us, "The first time I met our leadership team chair was when she gave a speech at our faculty orientation meeting in the fall. She really seemed uptight and formal. I was surprised at how much fun she could be when I got to know her." It is useful to remind ourselves that both persons and settings have personalities.

Give attention to ways that invite and fail to invite others to enter or not enter a network. A teacher leader was happily surprised when a message she sent to a leadership team member on e-mail over the weekend became part of that member's report to the faculty on Monday afternoon.

Give attention to ways that people invite or fail to invite others to enter or not enter a network. "We really need her expertise and should invite her to talk to us about the new reading program at our next leadership team meeting," one teacher leader said about a central office supervisor. "She has enough to do and really isn't that well received," said another teacher leader. Networking gives you access to information about the effectiveness of persons in organizations.

Be aware of the fact that some people will feel that your network contacts invade their territory. Informal relationships often tend to threaten persons who feel comfortable and secure with hierarchical relationships. These people will therefore find your networking threatening. "How can I run this department when the superintendent makes so many decisions on the golf course?" a director of personnel said.

Recognize the fact that some persons in the formal structure will participate in formal decision-making situations even though they know that the real decision making has occurred or will occur in informal networking situations. There are times when people play out their roles in formal situations knowing full well that important decisions are rarely made in such settings. Recognizing the importance of ritual can keep you from becoming cynical. Also, it is helpful to realize that you will be on the other end of this at times.

Give attention to the importance of how much information a person is willing to give about network contacts. The more information given, the higher the trust level.

Be aware of the fact that persons with formal positions of authority will still use old, informal networks to some extent. A principal in a new school was somewhat surprised to discover that teachers in her former school still called for advice. These teachers also had a hidden agenda: They wanted inside information as to what was going on in the central office.

Recognize that potential conflict between informal networking and "going through channels" exists. Once again, lateral decisions in a network threaten the command-compliance decision making in the bureaucratic hierarchy. Effective teacher leaders will be envied by some bureaucrats who think others don't know their place.

CONCLUSION

There have been several waves of school reform in the United States. Doris Henderson (personal interview, January 2005), former principal of Guilford Primary School in Greensboro, North Carolina, describes the characteristics of her school's teacher leaders:

> They are catalysts who are eager to share new ideas with each other. They are proactive and don't sit and wait for someone else to lead. They are excited about education and learning and have a way of spreading the gospel of the school and schooling. They are always open to learning, are constantly curious, and always seem to be asking questions. They are kind to children and ask them things that make them grow— the why questions. They are positive, can-do people who don't let things get them down. They are highly motivated hard workers who are always willing to go the extra mile. They know that flash and fads are no substitute for effective leadership, good teaching, and learning.
>
> Finally, they are strong models for all of the good things I've just mentioned about them. I was so proud to be their principal.

We hope that we have left you, the reader, with the feeling that being a teacher leader is a challenging and rewarding position in the school and the school system. In fact, it is the potential and real problems and dilemmas you face that will bring life to your leadership. To be a teacher leader is to have a vision of a better future. It is this hopefulness that is contagious in a school and a school system. It is this hopefulness that will help you both avoid and deal with derailment.

CHAPTER SEVEN

The Seasons of an Educational Leader's Career

*In every period we suffer because of the undone developmental
work of previous periods but we also have an opportunity to
do further developmental work and to create a life more suit-
able to the self.*

—D. Levinson (1985, p. 63)

The purpose of this capstone chapter is to place the
understandings you have arrived at in reading the first
six chapters of this book in the context of the seasons of an educational leader's career. This chapter will be a kind of refresher
course that will help you better understand where you have been
in your career while at the same time keeping an eye out for where
you want to be in the future. The four seasons we have identified
are: (a) preparing to become an educational administrator;
(b) entering educational administration; (c) settling in—the middle
years; and (d) the later years as an educational administrator.

No matter which stage you are presently at, you can profit
from reflecting on where you have been and where you are going.
The way in which each of us presents ourself as an educational

leader is an expression of both our view as to what we have previously experienced and our sense of who we are becoming as a person and leader. It is this process of becoming that brings vitality to our lives and leadership. This is expressed in the story of a young person who stopped at a gas station in a small town. "Have you lived here all of your life?" the old timer at the gas pump was asked. "Not yet," the man answered. His life was unfinished, as he was still in the process of becoming. As we look backward, we will have a clearer picture of those factors that have helped us stay on track in our career as well as those forces that have led us toward derailment. As we look forward, we are better able to develop career plans that will keep us on track and avoid or deal with derailment in a more effective way.

We have adopted a four-stage career structure that "consists of a series of alternating stable (structure-building) periods and transitional (structure-changing) periods" (Levinson, 1985, p. 49). You, the reader, will see that "a transitional period terminates the existing life structure and creates the possibility for a new one" (Levinson, 1985, p. 49). Termination is a loss, and as such can be very painful. If an educational leader learns to accept the realities of termination and sees these realities as part of the developmental process, individuation may occur with new understandings and leadership behaviors emerging.

There is a tug-of-war built into any career and life structure: "Even the best structure has its contradictions, and must in time be changed" (Levinson, 1985, p. 59). It is also the case that we will at times embrace separate and contradictory "truths." As a beginning educational administrator, for example, you are urged to keep options open and enjoy the sense of adventure at the same time that you are told that you must be responsible by representing and upholding the school as an organization. Levinson (1985) sends a warning shot across the beginning administrator's bow with regard to choices and the future: "If these choices are congruent with dreams, talents, and external possibilities, they provide the basis for a relatively satisfactory life structure. If the choices are poorly made and the new structure seriously flawed, you will pay a heavy price in the next period" (p. 59).

As the reader of this chapter, you may be a teacher, an assistant principal, a principal, a central office administrator, or a superintendent. In the event that you are a teacher, you may well be moving toward an administrative position in a school. If you have this in mind, you are probably already assuming teacher leader responsibilities. Whatever your present position and aspirations for the future, you will most likely begin the story of your career with childhood memories of what teachers and administrators do. These memories have provided you with an anticipatory set—a frame of mind to begin assessing, and perhaps playing, the role of teacher long before you were credentialed as a teacher. We will refer to this as *before the beginning—preparing the way.* (See Case 5, "What Kind of Superintendent Will I Be?" in the Resources section at the end of this book.)

PREPARING THE WAY TO BECOME AN EDUCATIONAL ADMINISTRATOR

Take a moment to go back in time to answer the following question: "What are the characteristics of one or more teachers who served as a positive role model?" Excerpts from graduate student career stories illustrate the contributions of inviting teachers:

> Ardis Snyder taught us during one of the most difficult years in our lives—the fifth grade. She inherited an unruly fourth grade class and turned it into a learning community with no classroom management problems. She loved teaching and we loved coming to class every day. She saw goodness and possibilities in us that we didn't see in ourselves.

> Mr. Miller was one of the most interesting persons I ever met. He didn't act as if he had all of the answers. In fact, he opened up our classroom to a world that we had never experienced and he acted as if he learned as much as we did. He came across as genuine and authentic rather than as a phony who always had to be right.

He loved science and would say things that stimulated thought. He came into our sixth-grade class one day with a picture of a casket. He said, "You know, class, I've been thinking of buying my casket early so that I can get some use out of it ahead of time. What kinds of things do you think I might do to use this before I die?" We listed all of the things we could think of, from storing apples to using it as a file cabinet. In the process, we had to consider where the casket should be stored, the weather conditions that were conducive to this or that activity, etc. This problem-solving situation became a mini-unit that taught us a good deal of science and more.

Now, ask yourself, "How would I describe one or more teachers who served as negative role models?" Graduate students' career stories revealed the following:

We learned to feed Mr. Crantz's ego from day one. He was an entertainer who obviously cared more about his performances than he did about our learning. In fact, I don't think he even knew the names of some of the students at the end of the year.

Ms. James was obviously bright and must have received good grades when she was a student. She simply wasn't cut out to be a teacher. The students took over the class. All Ms. James could talk about was how this would be her last year of teaching as she would go into business where she could make more money.

Ms. Allen had a system for everything. No one could criticize her for being disorganized. The problem for me was that she treated us like empty vessels to be filled with her ideas. She had what I would call a closed-system way of thinking. Everything important was already known to her, and it was her job to be sure that we learned it.

Some of you reading this chapter had a sense of calling or vocation that drew you to teaching from early childhood. An educator wrote, "My kindergarten teacher and I had the same last name, and so when I played school in the neighborhood, I was usually chosen to be the teacher. After school and during the summertime, my friends and I went to the playground and I was usually 'the teacher' during recess time. I knew that I wanted to be a teacher from the time I was five. In fact, I wanted to be one of the best, just like my best teachers." When you have this vision of doing great things, your sense of "calling will likely be worked out in ways that you currently can't even begin to imagine" (Peck, 1993, p. 70).

Some of you reading this book may have considered other vocations before turning to teaching. The important thing is that the effective teacher, like the proficient actor in the theater, wants to be with students in classrooms and other learning settings, and keeps this *passion for teaching* throughout his or her career (Goffman, 1959).

Passion for teaching is fueled by *passion for learning.* Educators who shared their career stories with us had vivid memories of the sense of awe, wonder, and amazement that they experienced as curious children exploring the world around them. They cited the following examples:

> My parents took me to an airport in Greensboro when I was 12 and I rode in an airplane to Charlotte without my parents. It was scary at first, but I had a real sense of accomplishment: "I can do this!" I used the memory of this to give me confidence to fly all around the United States as well as overseas when I became an adult.

> I remember the first day of school as a kindergartner—the sounds, smells, colors. The room was clean and neat and the teacher greeted me by name.

The forging of relationships as children was another kind of discovery and challenge. Attitudes and behaviors learned in the process became the foundation of cooperation and teaming that would last a lifetime. The thrill of such learning is evidenced in the following poem, written by Jerrika Ellinger when she was 12 years old:

Those Cousins of Mine

I was going to my cousins' house
On Thanksgiving Day.
We hadn't seen each other
And were too shy to play.
Once it came time to eat,
We started to talk.
We did magic tricks,
And even took a walk.
We watched movies
Like *Legally Blond 2* and *Rat Race.*
Then things got boring
At a fast pace.
We were the only two girls with five guys
That always wanted to play.
I didn't plan on staying the night
So I wore the same clothes for three days.
We went to the movies
To see Haunted Mansion.
We played spoons; it was so fun.
It got all of us dancin.'
We made quesadillas,
They were so yummy.
Her slobbering dog Bowie
Slobbered so yucky!
I love all my cousins;
I wish I could go back again.
And that is the story
Of my fantastic weekend.

(Jerrika Ellinger. Used with permission.)

A visitor to any elementary-school classroom can quickly grasp the authenticity and candor exhibited by children. It is the *zeitgeist* of the classroom, what is in the air, that those entering educational administration are afraid they will miss the most when they leave teaching. A beginning assistant principal captured this best: "I hope that I will never forget that one of the greatest gifts I can give those I lead is to build on the memory of what it was like to be a child curious about everything I experienced."

What is the context and purpose of the first 20 years of one's life? The overall shape of this period is that of "an incomplete, highly dependent child growing in complex, biological, psychological and social ways to become, in greater or lesser degree, an independent, responsible adult" (Levinson, 1985, p. 3). We have, during this time, the beginning steps in shaping a worldview, including a sense of place and time. And we can see the important role of significant persons, formal and informal education, and spiritual influences. Young persons are also beginning to assume a stance with regard to optimism, hopefulness, and pessimism. Although fantasies are created, the reality of the world around them tempers such fantasies. Without such a balance, young people will face a difficult future.

Nearly all principals have had teaching experience—something that gives them credibility with teachers when they become administrators. Learning to accept the professional responsibilities of the teacher is a challenge. Many teachers have shared with us stories about their first student-teaching experience—the first time most of them assumed teaching responsibility. A middle school teacher looked back on student teaching and shared the following narrative:

> Mr. Kitter, the master teacher who taught social studies, called in sick on a Monday morning in the fall early in my student-teaching experience. I was sitting in the back of the room correcting papers when the principal walked into the classroom and said that I would take over for the day. I had that "deer in the headlights" feeling and took the longest walk

I had ever taken in my life—from the back of the classroom to the front of the classroom.

I was now an actor, not simply a reactor, as I had been in my university classes. It was a warm morning and the windows in our third-story classroom were wide open. As I walked toward the lectern in the front of the room, I turned to my left and said to myself, "I have to make one of two choices: I can jump out the window or I can start teaching." I fumbled around and felt clumsy for a while, but with time began to feel more comfortable as a teacher that morning in the classroom. It was a turning point in my life and the beginning of my career as a teacher.

The beginning teacher has mixed feelings that affect her or his presentation of self. A teacher shared the following description of her early experiences as a teacher:

I spent a good deal of time preparing for the first day of school. My room was decorated in an inviting way with a bulletin board and wall hangings that were very attractive. *I was really excited about being a teacher until the children arrived. Then, I was simply overwhelmed with the reality of the situation.* I had to work through the anxieties associated with being a beginning teacher until I got into a schedule where I had confidence. It took several months before I began to feel comfortable.

In the back of most beginning teachers' minds, a question lurks: "Am I up to this challenge?" (Huberman, 1989, p. 33).

A school administrator shared the following: "I didn't realize it until I wrote my career story, but my early years as a teacher set the norms for my vocational growth and development. I didn't want to fail as a teacher and so I did everything I could to teach in an acceptable way—a way that would not be criticized by my principal, assistant principal and teacher leaders." This quotation captures the beginning teacher's quest for professional identity and worthiness. The teacher searches for stability or stabilization at the same time that he or she senses the excitement of exploration and wonderment (Huberman, 1989). This beginning period is a struggle for balance and a real challenge. The beginning teacher hears two tapes: (1) Keep your options open, "avoid strong commitments and maximize the alternatives"; and (2) "become more responsible and make something of your life" (Levinson, 1985, p. 58).

It is clear from the career stories we read as well as a review of research on teachers and teaching that three things are especially important to teachers: "*Flexibility* to teach adaptively, the importance of *relationships* with students for knowing them well and motivating them, and the critical need to *focus on learning* rather than on the implementation of procedures" (Darling-Hammond, 1997, p. 71). In other words, teachers who make a positive difference view teaching as more of an art than a science (Sarason, 1996).

Ironically, the research of Darling-Hammond (1997) revealed the following:

> Most teachers in our study felt that their views of good teaching were at odds with those of their school districts. The large majority (79 percent) described concerns for children and for learning as central to good teaching, but only 11 percent felt their school districts shared this view. Most (75 percent) felt that their school districts were more concerned with implementing specific teaching techniques tied to precise objectives and with diagnosing student deficiencies. (p. 83)

These research findings become especially important as teachers move into assistant principalships and are expected to carry out district-level mandates. Newly appointed school administrators are often seen as double agents—a conflicted role to be sure.

ENTERING EDUCATIONAL ADMINISTRATION

Teachers become educational administrators for a variety of reasons: more life space, as they are not limited to the classroom; financial rewards; and the opportunity to influence a larger audience (Brubaker, 1995). Assistant principals and principals often serve as mentors for teachers interested in school administration.

In the process, teachers are given leadership opportunities that help prepare them for administration.

There is no single pathway for entering educational administration, as demonstrated by the following story:

> I left teaching for an assistant principalship because there was a convergence of forces or challenges with opportunities. As a teacher and mother, I entered the assistant principalship somewhat later than my younger colleagues. My divorce provided me with the opportunity to learn to be independent for the first time in my life. A new special education program in the high school helped me develop skills in working with parents, teachers, and administrators. This led to my being named chair of the department, where I acquired political skills as well as other kinds of skills in dealing with administrators. This provided me with further encouragement from people to enter school administration.
>
> Experience, maturity, and leadership plus certification merged. My children graduated from high school, where I was involved with cross-country meets, soccer games, swim and track meets, cooking dinner, and monitoring homework. When they went away to college, I had to get a life. I became a curriculum coordinator at a middle school and started work on a master's degree in school administration (MSA). When I finished my MSA, I got a job as an assistant principal in a middle school. My hope is that when I get a principalship, most of the negative aspects of administration will not be as dreadful and I will also be concerned about assistant principals and their growth. I'll support them.

What are the negative aspects of the assistant principalship, the frustrations that make this position so taxing and subject the assistant principal to the possibility of derailment? Assistant principals shared the following:

> I have learned to make myself do things I don't like to do—particularly discipline. I don't, however, like the fact that I am

expected to do the "grunt work" and I'm not given the respect the position demands. I have to make a lot of decisions quickly. I feel like I should have a big sign on saying "POTENTIAL!" One of the hardest things about discipline is that many times the student's story is closer to reality than the teacher's story. If I support the student's version of the story, teachers involved quickly tell other teachers that I have challenged their authority.

My biggest annoyance is with bureaucratic structures and trivia. They wear me down and take me away from relating to teachers and students as persons. The present culture of accountability exerts political pressure on school administrators to demonstrate immediate quantitative measures of success. I feel like I am constantly challenged to think about and decide how to locate and relate to authority and I am also challenged to use power judiciously. Being at the bottom rung of the administrative ladder doesn't help.

I'm learning so much about communication—what to say, how to say it, and what not to say. I didn't pay much attention to this as a teacher, but I've learned the hard way what one of my educational administration professors said at the end of his university career: "I've never been sorry for anything I didn't say."

I'm less interested in power and politics than in getting important things done. But, I've learned that power and politics are central to administration.

I am nearly always the person in the middle—the person between the principal and the faculty, the person between the teacher and the student. I don't have the positional authority of the principal and I can't pretend to be a teacher. I am in a lonely place.

At the same time, many assistant principals find their position to be an exciting one:

Although I am an assistant principal in a high school that has traditionally had men in this role, I feel like I am plowing new ground and can be a peacemaker at times whereas a man could be considered to be "soft" in this role.

It is exciting to be in a position that introduces me to reforms across the country. My challenge is to share this excitement, to win over some teachers who are jaded and have little interest in change.

It is exciting to be in a position where I see a need, fill it, and see it work. For example, this morning I cooled down a student in the hall and helped all of us avert a major problem.

My challenge is to learn to pace myself so that I can have enough resources left over to really make a difference in the lives of students and teachers. I am doing my best to have interests outside of school that will help me keep the kind of freshness I need to reach those I lead. It is easy to become overwhelmed in this job, as we wear so many hats and have so many improvement plans to implement.

I've learned a lot in my position. One of the main things is how leaders above me use labels to categorize those who work for them. For example, the superintendent, associate superintendent, and principal introduce me to persons by saying one thing about me, such as "I would like you to meet Ms. Stuart, who has her degree from Wake Forest University." They do this with other people, too. The way a person is introduced tells him or her a lot about the value system or priorities of the person making the introduction.

One of the most challenging things I have learned about leadership and administration is the tremendous diversity of personalities of faculty and staff members. I noticed this to some degree as a teacher, but now I have to deal with these diversities as one of the leaders of the whole school. I've learned to see this challenge as something I really like about leadership—the reason being that I chose to be an administrator to make a difference in a larger arena.

Relating to authorities who do what we believe are unreasonable things can be a real challenge in the beginning years of one's administrative career. A first-year principal was enthused by a mini-grant system that afforded teachers the opportunity to improve curriculum in their schools. The young principal, unaware that the superintendent wanted a controlled and closed information system, suggested to him that copies of teachers' successfully funded mini-grant proposals be placed in a central office location so that next year's applicants could see how to write their proposals. The superintendent replied, "I don't think this would be a good idea because some of the wrong teachers might apply." The first-year principal quickly learned that most principals told the superintendent only what he wanted to hear—the result being that the stated vision statements for schools and the school system existed only on paper. They had no real meaning.

Many female administrators over the years wrote in their life stories about an agonizing dilemma: rural culture taught them to respect the authority of "good ol' boy" administrators, with whom they had a kind of uncle-niece relationship, but this was at odds with their new feminist consciousness and career aspirations—a consciousness fueled by critical theorist professors in administrator preparation programs at universities. Rural civilities were now seen by many female administrators as a way to get along and to keep women in their place. Favorite "uncles" were deferred to at social gatherings, but the workplace was seen in a different light.

Professional educators and organizations urged principals to assume leadership in curriculum and instruction. Principals were also expected to involve teachers in schoolwide decision making, including formulating and articulating organizational vision. It was no longer enough for the principal to have a clean building and good food in the cafeteria while delegating curriculum leadership to a lead teacher—usually a woman.

A new consciousness with regard to gender and ethnic background and related opportunities for employment were coupled with larger school systems created through merger. More women and African Americans moved into assistant principalships, principalships, and central office administrative positions. Formerly favored white males began to perceive themselves as part of an administrative underclass. They felt cheated as they approached the new millennium.

Today, superintendents, principals, and assistant principals are expected to do it all. School boards want to be involved in the decision making formerly entrusted to educators. State legislators and federal politicians want quick fixes and introduce top-down educational reforms in the name of accountability. When asked what percentage of their job is political, superintendents and principals who wrote career stories said, "Over 90%."

In summary, entering the profession as an assistant principal can be an unsettling change from being a teacher. At the same time, it is an opportunity to learn from constant challenges. Personal and institutional *busyness* is such a prevailing influence that beginning administrators have little time to reflect on sense of place, sense of time, and spiritual influences, They are being socialized by their informal education, their on-the-job training, without being conscious for the most part as to emerging views of optimism, hopefulness, and pessimism. Significant persons, such as principals and central office administrators, are leaving their imprint on assistant principals who are beginning to decide if they want to stay in the profession, if they want to stay in the role of assistant principal, or if they want to leave this role in order to seek a principalship or central office position—often as a curriculum specialist.

If the beginning educational administrator is reasonably certain he or she wants to stay in this profession, a sense of stabilization sets in and affiliation with an occupational community begins to take place. A worldview is emerging in the mind of the assistant principal—usually without him or her knowing it. There is a new world aborning for most school administrators during their beginning years. The challenge is to survive creatively, stay on track, and avoid derailment. (See Case 2, "Assistant Principal Expected to Run School," in the Resources section at the end of this book.)

SETTLING IN—THE MIDDLE YEARS

The beginning season of an educator's career is often marked by "the dream"—an idealized vision as to what life will be like when one uses his or her talents to reach a high level of achievement and satisfaction (Goffman, 1959). Veterans in schools or school systems expect the beginner to pay his or her dues, much as they had to when they were neophytes. As one settles in during the middle years, it becomes clear that the distance between the dream and reality must be faced.

What are the options for the person who has not achieved the dream? First, the administrator can simply bide his or her time and try to ride it out until retirement. A career assistant principal voiced this position: "Don't appear to say 'no,' but rather redirect the invitation to give the inviter a piece of the pie. Just say things like, 'I'll be glad to serve on this committee, but I don't think I am the person to chair it.'" A second option is a somewhat risky one: become jaded or bitter. This clearly sends the signal that you are not and don't want to be on the team. Unless you have a talent that no one else has, you will be headed for derailment and demotion.

A third option is to squarely face those weaknesses your bureaucratic superiors see in you and do whatever you can to turn such weaknesses into strengths. This may require your moving into a different position in the organization—one that will value your talents while you work to improve your leadership skills. To deal with these matters well is to work smarter rather than simply harder or longer.

Midcareer autobiographers cite this understanding as one of the benefits of administrative experience. "I have gained confidence because I now have a history and have gained trust from children, teachers, staff, parents and others," one midcareer school administrator shared. This educational leader now sees connections not previously seen: "People learn best when they make connections between what they already know and what they are learning, when they can draw on their experiences and make greater meaning of them, when they can see how ideas relate to one another, and when they can use what they are learning in concrete ways" (Darling-Hammond, 1997, p. 55).

The settling-in period is a challenge for many educational leaders: "It was my time during the settling-in stage to make decisions—the job, where to live, etc. I've had guilt about this as a woman, wife, and mother. I had to redefine place, my sense of place, as I had no place to belong for a while. I was unsettled in trying to settle in."

We had the opportunity to observe a mid-career high school principal who was going through a kind of mid-life crisis with regard to what he did and did not want to do with his career and life. Mike was an administrative intern, and so I had a chance to go backstage in his life in order to see what he was truly experiencing. Mike didn't have the enthusiasm of the beginner, nor the clear vision of a person nearing retirement. Here is his story:

It's Monday morning and Mike hits the snooze button on his clock radio three times before swinging one leg out of bed, hoping the other will follow. He moves to the kitchen hoping that a glass of orange juice will wake him up, only to spill it on the floor. After running the dishrag across the floor, the juice still sticks to his feet. Mike knows this is going to be another one of those days.

After performing his morning ritual, Mike gets in his car and drives toward the high school in order to arrive two hours before the students. As he approaches the circular drive in front of the school, an amazing thing happens. His car simply moves around the circle and heads toward home. He says to himself, "I won't do anybody any good today. I'm going home. I'll call in sick." He parks his car in the garage, walks into the house, and crawls back into bed. Half an hour later, Mike gets dressed and returns to school, this time parking his car in its usual space, and enters the building. Sitting behind his desk, Mike starts softly singing John Lennon's 1980 hit, "Watching the Wheels." After singing, "I tell them there's no hurry, I'm just sitting here doing time," Mike stops, smiles, and wonders what it would take to reclaim the fire he once had.

Mike's story is probably one any experienced school administrator can understand. Facing the reality of your leadership abilities and the settings in which you work can be a very challenging task. A principal said, "All of the idealistic slogans and promises from my early years as an administrator are being challenged and this is sobering: 'You not only can but must reach everyone.' 'Every person can learn what you, the principal, care enough about to "teach" as you lead.'" The principal added, "Much of the freshness and energy of the beginning season is eroded and yet I can't see an end to my vocation and the pressures or stresses I will face until I do retire."

Midcareer administrators who wrote their life stories also cited the stress from seeing their own children through college at the same time that their parents were aging and needed more resources—emotional and often financial. A woman in her mid-forties described her situation as a principal in the middle period of her career: "It is clear to me that I can't constantly bounce from one position to another, but must instead face sustained responsibility. At the same time, the reality of downsizing, outsourcing, and limited tenures in the principalship and superintendency must be faced." She added, "There seem to be fewer problems that can be solved and more dilemmas that have to be reconciled."

A principal in his late forties described his situation as follows:

My ship is already more than half way across the ocean with neither shore quickly reached. If I want a doctorate, the union card to university teaching, I have to get it as soon as possible. If I want to try to be a superintendent of schools, I had better become an assistant and associate superintendent in the next few years. It is clear to me that I seem to have unlimited desires and limited resources. And, along with the sense

of limited time, I also seem to be much more introspective—
something that often ties me in knots. The one thing that
I know for sure is that the secret to keeping the fire is to
continue to be turned on to learning.

Educational leaders in the midcareer stage have a clearer
sense of place vocationally and geographically. Many feel *place-
bound* due to a variety of factors: the position held by a spouse or
significant other; the difficulty of not having an advanced university degree; not having the support of bureaucratic superiors;
physical or emotional disabilities; the need to be near their
children, parents, or relatives; and the love for and comfort in staying in a geographic area. Coming to terms with one's sense
of place can be one of the most challenging and rewarding
aspects of the midcareer stage. Significant persons within and
outside of education can play an important role in supporting the
midcareer educational leader. To not have this kind of support is to
risk loneliness and depression.

One's sense of time during the midcareer phase is often a
mixed feeling. At one moment, it may seem as if there is no end to
work and career, while at another moment, one wonders at how
fleeting one's life has been and feels there will never be enough
time to do all of the things one wants to do. Difficult decisions and
commitments must be made, for example, if one wants to achieve
a more formal education that will open up opportunities for
advancement in school or school-system administration or higher
education.

As the midcareer educational leader assesses time and place,
there is often a reaching out for spiritual meaning. The role of
spiritual growth and religious institutions in the lives of the
children we love has been acted out on the stage of life and can be
assessed, often compared to one's own experiences at their age.
And, for some midcareer educators, the loss of parents and other
older loved ones confronts them with the reality of letting go and
the impending end of career and life itself.

All of these matters obviously influence one's view of
optimism, hopefulness, and pessimism. One doctoral student's
comment in a career story, voluntarily shared with the class,

stimulated a good deal of discussion: "I was just thinking lately that there is no hospital named 'The City of Optimism.' Given my experiences in life, I am now more hopeful than optimistic." Students also talked a good deal about how important it is during the midcareer to be able to honestly share their emotions and feelings about optimism, hopefulness, and pessimism. The role of community and the stages of community building are important in this whole process (Brubaker, 2004).

Finally, the educational leader's worldview often begins to take shape and become more sophisticated during the midcareer stage. Graduate classes can provide the opportunity for this to take place. The kind of writing of career stories that has been discussed in this book serves as an example. Increased attention to informal education, such as conversations with mentors and other older educators and noneducators, can also be important in shaping one's worldview.

Observing older colleagues in the recessional stage of their careers can also be very instructive. It is during the latter part of the midcareer stage that some educational leaders begin to grasp the significant difference between information and wisdom. In separating the wheat from the chaff, the educational leader learns the important role of discernment. We asked a career assistant principal what the most important thing was that he learned during his 25-year career. He responded,

I had rickets as a child and I walk with a slight limp. When I began my career as an assistant principal, I would walk down the hall and a boy after passing me would occasionally mimic my limp. I would turn around and have him up against the wall. I learned with time what to see and what not to see, what to act upon and what not to act upon. I no longer operate as a kind of warden always looking for someone doing something wrong. I can be firm but fair, and I have learned to celebrate things that students do right and what students learn from what they do wrong.

There are two major tasks during the settling in career stage: to establish a niche in your career, a place where you "develop competence in a chosen craft, become a valued member of a valued world, and "striving to advance, to progress on a timetable" (Levinson, 1985, p. 59). Levinson (1985) adds: "The imagery of the ladder is central to the Settling Down period enterprise. It reflects the interest in advancement so central to this period" (p. 59). What does Levinson mean by the ladder? He is referring "to all dimensions of advancement—increases in social rank, income, power, fame, creativity, quality of family life, and social contribution" (Levinson, 1985, p. 59).

It is during the settling-in career stage that the educational leader often acquires important wisdom about staying on track and avoiding or dealing with derailment. In earlier stages, one has the tendency to run away from these realities rather than facing them and making necessary adjustments.

THE LATER YEARS AS AN EDUCATIONAL ADMINISTRATOR

"The sunset years of an educational leader's career are a time to assess past performances and focus on the things that really interest me," according to a veteran administrator. He continued,

> There is no need to compete, nothing to prove. Sometimes, I just look hard at a person and say to myself, "He's just trying to find his way—just like me," whereas in the past I would have said, "I've got to do everything I can to change him." I've learned that I can make changes in my own life that may or may not lead to basic changes in the lives of those I lead. I can't force others over the bridge, but I can act in such a way that they see an example of one way to cross the bridge.

Issues of staying on track and avoiding or dealing with derailment are often simply beside the point—out of sight and out of mind with regard to one's own career.

Those educators in the recessional season of their careers often have a clear view as to the attitudes and behaviors they presently have, in contrast to the earlier years in their lives, when they were less aware. As a result, they share with others things that younger colleagues are reluctant to share. Arthur M. Schlesinger, Jr. (2000), renowned Harvard historian and special assistant to President John F. Kennedy, writes,

> Although I now rather enjoy lecturing, I never quite escaped the impostor complex, the fear that I would one day be found out. My knowledge was by some standards considerable, but it was outweighed by my awareness of my ignorance. I always saw myself skating over thin ice. The impostor complex had its value. It created a great reluctance, for example, to impose my views on students. (p. 439)

Schlesinger's statement reminds us that a sense of humility often sets in during the later years in one's career. One recognizes that certitude plus limited knowledge during the earlier years often produced arrogance. We learn by turning in the dictionary to the word *creed* from the Latin *credo*—meaning to "set the heart"—that one does not know for certain, but instead hopes something is true (Adams, 1983).

Some administrators in the fourth career stage write about how they now have more time for spiritual growth, family, and friends. "The challenge I face is to let go of the things that matter less to me," a principal wrote. She explained,

> When I began as a principal, I would get to school early and do the things the custodians had overlooked. Then, I did some of the things the secretary usually forgets to do before she gets to work. I would then move to the cafeteria to be sure that all of the details were taken care of there. Finally, I went from classroom to classroom to neaten up some of the things for teachers who tended to be sloppy. It has been hard psychological work for me to let go of these things that I controlled so well. I now see that I denied some of these people the opportunity to do better work. I was treating them like I treated my children.

For some veteran educational administrators, this is the most fulfilling time in their lives. "They are less tyrannized by the ambitions, passions and illusions of youth. They can be more deeply attached to others and yet more separate, more centered in the self" (Levinson, 1985, p. 62).

Another principal in the latter years of the recessional career stage shared her appreciation for reflection and connection:

> There is a smoothness to my life now in contrast to my earlier years in school administration. There is more grace and less pace in the way I do things. I'm taking time to reflect before I act and, as a result, I feel like I am connecting more with others and how they are experiencing the school as an environment. I'm seeing things through their eyes more rather than manipulating them to do what needs to be done.

In order for this principal to have these insights, she had to sense some "letting go," of disengagement (Huberman, 1989).

A central office administrator shared the following dialogue she had with a younger bureaucratic superior who asked her to do some extra work. "'No,' I said. 'I'm not interested in doing that.' 'But, we all have to pull our load,' she responded. I just smiled and she stopped asking me to do extra things. This was a turning point in our relationship."

Many veteran administrators referred to diminished physical capabilities. One described his plight: "I never thought I would end up this way. I was always an active, independent person, but now some health problems have forced me to rely on others more. I have mixed feelings about this—a sense of freedom, but also some guilt." This administrator added, "I am reminded of my grandmother's admonition about old age: 'If you sit down, you may not get up.'"

It is a challenge for those who feel despair to find antidotes that bring light into their darkness. Connectedness best describes what can help in such situations (Barth, 2003). Friendship, family, and meaningful work can make a difference. Some educators in this season of life begin turning to activities they want to pursue when they retire. A principal who lived four hours from the ocean found that she and her husband went to their beach house almost every weekend during her last year as a principal. Another principal repeated the words of her travel agent: "See the world before you leave it, because many leave it before they see it."

Other administrators near retirement age turn to mentoring younger administrators as a way to give something back to schools and school systems. A principal described her mentoring of assistant principals and teacher leaders:

> Mentoring is a somewhat tricky business. The mentee has to be ready for this kind of help. The mentee almost always approaches the mentor for help. Once the mentee really learns to do things well, the relationship with the mentor changes, and this is sometimes difficult for the mentor to accept. I am sensitive to this and like the idea that I have a kind of legacy in helping younger colleagues if they want me to help them. Mentoring, to me, is using my talents to help others identify and use their talents.

Since staying on track and avoiding derailment is of little interest or consequence for most leaders nearing retirement, the mentor can help younger colleagues deal with these issues in a nonthreatening way.

An associate superintendent responsible for curriculum and instruction shared her observation of educators nearing retirement:

> A few years ago, I began to notice how different colleagues treat the years just before they retire. I probably did this because I was at the end of the middle of my career and wondered how I would deal with the years just before I retired. I observed that some educators act as if they have arrived at some kind of inner peace. For example, a kind of gentleness and even sweetness comes over some previously aggressive men. They have shared with me an appreciation for their colleagues' contributions and stories about how much they

enjoy being with their grandchildren. Sometimes, I feel as if they are trying to rectify errors of omission from earlier years in their lives and careers. One man said to me, "I've never heard a retiree say that he spent too little time at work, but I have heard a lot of them say that they didn't spend enough quality time with their children and friends."

She added, "However, I have also noticed some educators who are very angry and jaded. They simply counted the years before they could retire and many would share their desire to no longer be there. I didn't enjoy being around these people and vowed to do whatever I could not to be this way when I reached this time in my career."

Educational administrators and teachers who are stuck in anger lose their credibility and waste their resources and those of the people they are expected to lead. When a leader's anger is prolonged, people in their company recognize that their anger will not be channeled into something productive. It is simply self-absorbed venting.

The attitudes and actions described in this section of the chapter describe some veteran educational leaders who have achieved insights that demonstrate a more complete worldview. They have fashioned lives that illustrate an understanding of their sense of place and time. They have experienced a kind of comfort that leads to an appreciation of significant persons in their personal and professional lives and to an honest assessment of the attitudes and behaviors of those who have influenced them for better or worse. They have learned to concentrate on the good things and look past the disappointments. Hopefulness replaces an optimism based on fantasies that have little connection with the realities of career and life itself. Formal education takes a backseat to informal learning acquired in settings with little, if any, bureaucratic pressure.

For these veterans, lateral relationships are more the norm, with command-compliance relationships avoided if at all possible. For many, this recessional stage affords opportunities for spiritual growth never imagined during earlier career and life stages. And, taking the time to authentically engage in the civilities of leadership—observing, celebrating, and acting on the goodness of others—allows and encourages us to appreciate such qualities in ourselves. They realize that "authentic performance is critical to the development of competence. Thus, meaningful performances in real-world contexts need to become both the stuff of the curriculum and the focus of assessment events" (Darling-Hammond, 1997, p. 115). Those who have not achieved these insights may well find that they take destructive attitudes and actions into retirement with them.

CONCLUSION

There are seasons in an educator's career much like the seasons in any person's life (Levinson, 1985). Thinking and/or writing about these seasons can be an important way to understand one's self and others better. With this understanding comes the ability to celebrate those things that are working well in an educational leader's life and also a chance to explore alternative ways of doing things that benefit one's self and the organization. It is one's sense of becoming a better person and leader that inspires and empowers. "I *can* make a difference" becomes "I *will* make a difference by doing the following things." The confidence that is gained through such thinking and acting increases one's competence—a gift to self and the organization. In the process, others learn from our example.

Afterword

In the time since the initial publication of *Staying on Track*, we have been fortunate to receive many letters, e-mails, and comments that have clarified and extended ideas in our writing. The five reviewers of the manuscript for the second edition have also helped us see things that have been immensely helpful. In this Afterword, we want to share some of their thoughts as well as some new insights we have acquired in order to bring the second edition of *Staying on Track* to a successful conclusion.

A good deal of attention has been given in recent years to the purpose-driven life in general and careers in particular. Reviewers tell us that the second edition of *Staying on Track* makes a distinct contribution to the field by speaking to current and aspiring administrators, as well as to professors of educational administration, about the management of their careers within the context of a purpose-driven life. A principal at a leadership conference writes, "A principal colleague is sitting with me in the hotel lobby, reading the loose-leaf manuscript pages as I put them down. As we read, we frequently stop to talk about points made in the book and how they relate directly to us as we consider voluntary career moves for next school year."

Another reviewer writes about the power of narrative in *Staying on Track:*

> The "cautionary tale" about a teacher leader moving up the ladder by becoming an assistant principal, principal, and then superintendent is a compelling narrative in which my colleagues and I immediately identify with the content of the book. The self-assessment checklists are riveting and provide

opportunities for reflection by evaluating others' actions as well as our own. The authors don't simply talk at us, but invite us to share our experiences, perceptions, and reflections.

A letter from another principal focuses on the relationship between staying on track and derailment:

> The authors are realistic about the challenges we face as educational leaders and they are always hopeful by citing ways in which we can deal with problems and dilemmas. They provide a map for career success and for helping those we lead. The can-do tone of the book is refreshing! They share the message, "Now that you know this, here's what to do with it." The book is inspirational!

A reviewer, caught up in the busy world of a high school principal, took time to write about the importance of caring and encouragement:

> With nine years of administration behind me, the last four years as a high school principal have at times been over-whelming due to constant demands and expectations. This book provides worthwhile and efficient strategies that I can easily implement into my daily routine to assist me in main-taining focus with positive energy. The case studies and other resources at the end of the book will be invaluable as a vehicle for problem solving, creating dialogue, and evaluating all components of decision making.

As the authors of this book, we appreciate and celebrate your entering into conversations with us as we work together to create better schools and lives for our students and colleagues. As in the Preface, we invite you to continue our conversations by e-mailing us at dlbrubak@uncg.edu and lrrycble@bellsouth.net

Resources

We have developed a number of resources that have aided us in leading seminars on the derailment issue. These resources may be read and reacted to privately or in a group setting. They speak to a number of themes connected to both avoiding and dealing with derailment: communication, shared decision making, working as a team, effective leadership, community building, interpersonal relationships, sources of power, personal disclosure, and risk taking.

The major part of this resource section consists of cases, which, as we have said earlier, are the next best thing to being there. These cases will make it clear that there are no quick fixes and simple answers to the complex situations in which educational leaders find themselves. In fact, cases provoke a good deal of discussion because of their complexity.

The format of the cases presented is that each case will be followed by alternative responses, after which the best possible rationale for each response is given. We also give our opinion as to what the best answer is. We invite you to revise this format so that it works for you, given the particular situation in which you find yourself. Please fill in blank spaces when they appear in some resources.

RESOURCE A: QUESTIONS IMPORTANT TO EDUCATIONAL LEADERS WHO WANT TO AVOID OR DEAL WITH DERAILMENT

As an educational leader interested in avoiding derailment—or in dealing with derailment when it happens—ask yourself the following questions:

1. In whose interest is this decision? [Who profits?]

2. Whose ox is gored? [Who suffers?]

3. How shall we live together? [The constitutional issue.]

4. How shall I live with myself? [The personal issue.]

5. How is critique helpful in this situation? [*Critique* is summary, adoption of a point of view, and gathering supportive evidence for this point of view.]

6. What is the transactional context and how does it influence persons and organizations involved?

7. What is the core of my work?

8. Who defines the core of my work? [If I enjoy the core of my work, I feel good about my work and myself.]

9. How can I survive creatively if my superordinate has an outside in, "get the glory" approach?

10.

11.

12.

13.

14.

15.

RESOURCE B: ENTRANCE AND EXIT RITUALS

This inventory is designed for you to write notes about entrance and exit rituals that do exist and should exist in the setting in which you give leadership.

What entrance rituals *presently exist* in the setting in which you give leadership? What entrance rituals *should exist* in the setting in which you give leadership?

1.

2.

3.

What exit rituals *presently exist* in the setting in which you give leadership? What exit rituals *should exist* in the setting in which you give leadership?

1.

2.

3.

Entrance and Exit Rituals (Completed Example)

This completed inventory serves as an example of how one seminar participant responded to the previous inventory.

What entrance rituals *presently exist* in the setting in which you give leadership? What entrance rituals *should exist* in the setting in which you give leadership?

1. Principal enters the room to greet parents and others, shakes hands, and has good eye contact. (Keep this practice and continue to model and discuss it.)

2. Principal has good energy and shares vision for the school. (Continue this behavior.)

3. Principal has high counter that separates guests from secretaries and self. (Remove counter. Offer guests coffee. Shake hands and have good eye contact.)

4. An assistant principal born and raised in Mexico was hired. He wants welcoming signs in Spanish and English in front of the school. He also has a list of other things that will make Spanish-speaking persons, especially parents and relatives, welcome in the school. (Support the assistant principal in any way possible.)

What exit rituals *presently exist* in the setting in which you give leadership? What exit rituals *should exist* in the setting in which you give leadership?

1. Principal and others walk parents and guests out school door. (Continue to encourage this.)

2. Good things going on at school are discussed with parents and others as they leave the building. (Continue to encourage this.)

3. Parents and guests are invited back, and interest is shown in them and their children. (Continue to encourage this. Have a professional development program for teachers in which these practices are discussed.)

RESOURCE C: WORKING ALONE
AND WORKING WITH A TEAM

A school and school system based on democratic tenets recognizes and values autonomy (working alone) and working as part of a team. It is a challenge to each leader to find the most satisfying balance between these two ways of operating.

We have found the following exercise helpful in that it promotes honest communication as to how each person has fashioned a professional life that includes working alone and working with others on a team.

Please complete the following paragraphs:

1. There are times when I enjoy working alone. Some of these times are . . .

    _____

    _____

    _____

    _____

2. Some of the reasons why I enjoy working alone are . . .

    _____

    _____

    _____

    _____

3. There are times when I don't enjoy working alone. Instead, I want to be with others as part of a team. Some of these times are . . .

    _____

    _____

    _____

    _____

4. Some of the reasons why I enjoy working on a team are . . .

_____

_____

_____

_____

How do you know when you're a team member? Place make a check mark in front of the items you support.

1. I recognize that what I do affects others on the team as well as those the team influences—for example, students.

2. No one on the team projects the feeling that he or she is better than others.

3. I am privately willing to acknowledge other team members' talents and contributions.

4. I rarely feel lonely.

5. I rarely feel down but instead feel lifted up by other team members and those I influence.

6. I feel energized.

7. I discover human and nonhuman resources I didn't know I had.

8. I have the courage to do what is right.

9. My vision for the future is sharpened, thus motivating myself and others.

10. I can agree and disagree with team members without taking this personally.

RESOURCE D: CONTRADICTIONS

Contradiction comes from the Latin *contra* (against) + *dicere* or *dictus* (to say). A contradiction is defined as the act of saying the opposite of something already said.

Two kinds of contradictions facing the educational leader are the basis for the following exercise. These contradictions are (1) those one chooses to celebrate and (2) those one chooses to try to reconcile. (We talk about problem *solving* and dilemma *reconciling.*)

Please identify below those contradictions that you face as a leader and celebrate. Then identify those contradictions that you choose to try to reconcile:

Column 1(celebrate)   Column 2 (reconcile)

Completed Example

Following are examples of the two kinds of contradictions facing the educational leader:

Column 1(celebrate)	Column 2 (reconcile)
"We have excellent parent involvement, and this means we give many of our resources (e.g., time and effort) to parents."	"I always feel like I'm the person in the middle."
"I appreciate the energy of young colleagues."	"There are always more desires (wants) than resources, but many are really about what I as principal can and can't do."

"Because I have a proven track record, people call on me to do more than I sometimes want to do."

"Some teachers nag, which I don't like, and yet I admire their commitment."

"I support the importance of accountability but I resent the fact that high-stakes tests and testing have been mandated."

"As a woman administrator, I always confront (have to deal with) the 'ol' boys club.'"

RESOURCE E: CONTRADICTIONS
FACING THE EDUCATIONAL LEADER

The following list articulates some of the contradictions currently facing educational leaders:

- *Professional autonomy* versus *state regulation and supervision*
- *"You are the professional with expertise"* versus *"Outside consultants are the experts"*
- *Competition with other schools* versus *cooperation with other schools*
- *Display accomplishments* versus *quietly go about your business*

Your challenge is to reconcile these contradictions. They are dilemmas you have to live with rather than problems that can be solved. Which of the following metaphors describe how you feel about this decision-making reality?

- Herding cats?
- Juggling?
- Steering a dog by moving its tail?

RESOURCE F: CASE STUDIES

Case 1: Getting on Track

After getting your undergraduate teaching degree with a major in science, you teach for three years and then decide to get a master's degree in educational administration with a minor in science education. After receiving your administrative certification, you apply for assistant principalships year after year, to no avail. In fact, during this five-year interval, you have been interviewed for only one assistant principalship.

You are happy as a teacher but really want to see what it would be like to be an assistant principal. You are also well aware that an administrative job would give you a higher salary and more life space. Because you live in a somewhat urban area, you would be willing to drive for up to one hour each way to take an assistant principalship, if it were offered.

Before you apply outside your system or give up your administrative dream, you talk to a friend who is principal in your system. You say, "Please give me honest feedback as to why you think I haven't had more interviews or been given an offer of an assistant principalship." Your friend pauses and replies, "I will give you honest feedback if this is off the record, but I don't want this getting back to central office and the director of personnel. Do you still want the feedback?"

You gulp but push on, agreeing to the conditions your friend has stated. Your friend speaks in a straightforward but caring way:

> You are known as a really fine teacher whose interest in students and science has made you highly respected. But principals and central office administrators simply don't see you as an administrator. You dress in an informal and somewhat sloppy way, and your classroom looks like a mess even though you can find things when you need them. There are times when your classroom smells from all the animal cages in it. Your problem is one of image. You don't look like an administrator. Until you change this image, you won't get interviews and job offers.

After considering your friend's advice, you recognize that you have several alternatives from which to choose:

1. Give up your dream of becoming an assistant principal and continue to be a respected classroom teacher.

2. Continue to apply for assistant principalships in and near your present school system, but don't make any effort to follow your friend's advice.

3. Take your friend's advice: Change your image and teaching behaviors so that they are consistent with your new image, and apply for assistant principalships in your system.

4. Take your friend's advice: Change your image and teaching behaviors so that they are consistent with your new image, and apply for assistant principalships in nearby systems.

Case 1: Rationales for Alternative Responses

1. The key to your effective teaching is your authenticity. Your teaching style, including your informal dress and seemingly disorganized classroom, is part of who you are. In the classroom setting, it works. Don't try to be something or someone you aren't. It is better to give up your dream of being an administrator. This may be the best choice if you are basically happy as a classroom teacher and don't want to make changes suggested by your friend.

2. Staying on the same path has the benefit of your keeping your authenticity; however, it is not likely that interviews or administrative job offers will be forthcoming.

3. Following your friend's advice will be hard work and you will feel uncomfortable at times as you change some of your personal behaviors, such as having a neater, better organized classroom. However, you have invested financial and other resources in getting your master's degree and certification in educational administration without having the opportunity to see how you like administration. The advantage of continuing to apply in your own system is

that you won't give up the comfort zone that system gives you, and, furthermore, you will probably have to make the changes in your classroom anyway, because other systems will call your principal and others to get a reading on the kind of teacher and educator you are. This response is one of two or three best choices.

4. Changing your image and applying to other systems nearby is a good choice because you will get a fresh start in other systems, whereas some people in your system will always retain the image of you they have had for years. However, you will be making several changes at the same time, and that can drain your psychological resources. This is an option, however, that is certainly worth examining carefully.

Case 2: Assistant Principal Expected to Run School

You have served as a teacher leader in a school while at the same time getting your master's degree and principal certification. Due to your excellent record in this school, the associate superintendent for curriculum and instruction has recommended you for an assistant principalship in the same school. You recently received this appointment by the board of education.

The problem is that the principal expects you to run the school. The principal was a coach and then driver's training instructor, and he has no interest or expertise in curriculum. Furthermore, the principal is rarely in the building between the time children get off the buses in the morning and the time when the buses leave in the afternoon. The principal does personal business throughout the day and is "somewhere between the school and central office," according to the secretary, who is an old friend and neighbor of the principal. The principal is frequently out with "the flu," and you sometimes smell alcohol on his breath during the school day.

The principal has 27 years in the retirement system and has made it clear that he will retire in three years.

What will you do? Please choose from the following alternatives:

1. Say nothing and go about your business in the most efficient way possible.

2. Do the best job you can, but be sure that the associate superintendent of curriculum and instruction understands that you are running the school and the principal has serious problems.

3. Do the best job you can and talk to a few trusted teachers and parents about the principal's problems so that they can support you if things become too difficult.

Case 2: Rationales for the Alternative Responses

1. This response has the virtue of not making waves. You will be recognized by those who count for your excellent work. The difficulty with this position is that, if the principal makes a serious mistake, you will be asked why you didn't say anything prior to that time. Seek a better response.

2. The associate superintendent of curriculum and instruction is your advocate, as evidenced by the fact that you were supported for this position. If any action is to be taken by your superordinates, the associate superintendent will be fully apprised of your situation. If the principal crosses the line and makes a serious mistake, the associate superintendent will also be informed of your situation. If you share your difficulties with only the associate superintendent, people will probably not call you indiscreet and unprofessional for gossiping. This is probably the best choice.

3. You will feel better in the short run for talking to teachers and parents—but you will probably pay a high price. The word will quickly get around that you are unprofessional and a gossip. This is a poor choice.

Case 3: Principal Hears New Superintendent's Views on Dress

You are having lunch with the new superintendent before the school year begins. The superintendent says, "You can't convince me that people don't sense whether or not you're professional from the minute they see how you're dressed. Good ol' boy principals usually wear short-sleeved shirts, rather than suits or sharp sport coats, and they often wear outdated ties. Women principals who dress inappropriately also come across as unprofessional." Now that you know your new superintendent's views on these matters, how will you act as principal with regard to them? Choose from among the following responses or add a better response of your own:

1. A principal's competence is what counts. Does he or she deliver? Dress is a personal and idiosyncratic matter. Continue to dress as you have.

2. Make minor adjustments in your dress if they are called for.

3. Follow the new superintendent's dress code.

Case 3: Rationales for the Alternative Responses

1. Dress is your own business and has nothing to do with success as a principal. You have demonstrated that you have done the job well, and people know that. The products of your work are what are really important. Don't openly confront the superintendent, but go about your business as you always have done, knowing full well this may be a major irritant to the superintendent. This may not be a good rationale, but it may be the rationale for a strong-headed person.

2. You will be a minor irritant on occasion to the superintendent, but you surely won't get into trouble that you would get into with the first response. Have clothes that are in style, whenever possible, but dress according to what makes you comfortable as much as you can. Be sure to dress appropriately for big occasions when the superintendent wants to show off the staff to the board and the community. Consider the next alternative.

3. Dressing correctly in the superintendent's eyes is a small price to pay for the good results you will achieve. Many

people will remember the impression you make with your clothes more than anything else. You are more likely to move up the ladder and be a successful administrator if you follow the superintendent's advice. Dress is symbolic, a kind of emotional shorthand, and as such it becomes an important matter to superintendents as they relate to principals. Superintendents want the organization and themselves to look good and appear to be winners.

Case 4: New Superintendent Edges You Out of Position

You are a 20-year veteran of a fairly large system and have worked your way through the ranks of teacher, assistant principal, and principal to become assistant superintendent for curriculum for the past five years. You and your spouse, a prominent attorney in the area, have high credibility in the community and the school system.

The system has been the scene of tremendous controversy, with several superintendents and split boards in recent years. You, however, have not only survived but also been a favorite of the past two superintendents due to your expertise and loyalty to these superintendents. Things have suddenly changed with the appointment of a young, out-of-state superintendent by a 5-to-2 vote of the board. The new superintendent quickly announces a restructuring plan, which will bring a deputy superintendent from the former school system into your system as the new deputy superintendent in charge of personnel, operations, and curriculum. The superintendent announces this to the press, saying that two assistant superintendencies will be eliminated, thus saving taxpayers more than $100,000. You are offered the position of director of staff development for one year, if you wish to look for another job, or permanently, if you wish to stay with the system.

What will you do? Please choose from the following options:

1. Resign and look for employment elsewhere.

2. Take the position as director of staff development and look for another assistant superintendency.

3. Take the position of director of staff development and ride it out until your retirement in a decade or less.

4. Use every source of power at your disposal to fight the new superintendent and the decision to derail you.

Case 4: Rationales for the Alternative Responses

1. Resigning will give you the immediate satisfaction of getting out of a system in turmoil. It will also make a public statement concerning your views of the new superintendent. However, you will probably be out of work for a year or longer as it will take time to get a new position—even if you use your contacts with two previous superintendents to get a job. It also will be difficult for you to relocate, given the rural district in which you live and your family commitments. Please consider a better option.

2. Taking the offer of the director of staff development will give you one year to decide if you want to seek employment elsewhere or reach an accommodation with the new superintendent. However, given the turmoil in the system, and your reading of the leadership style of the new superintendent, you will probably be in for a year that is very, very difficult. Essentially, you will get a salary but have no power or influence on the new superintendent and deputy superintendent. This is probably one of two best choices.

3. Taking the job of director of staff development and riding it out until retirement will assure you of a salary, but financial security will be won at a high price. It will probably be devastating, given the fact that you won't respect your superordinates and could well not want to be at work much of the time. Continue to search for a better answer.

4. Using all of the resources at your disposal can certainly make things hot for the new superintendent and deputy superintendent. You have high credibility in the community and can use the media, especially the local newspaper, to state your case. Also, your spouse could well announce candidacy for the school board when the next election takes place. Your spouse can also apprise you of your legal recourses each step of the way. While you are making your public protest, you can use your contacts

with the two previous superintendents, who are now located in other communities in the state, to get an assistant superintendency, central office leadership position, or principalship. You may have to live in another community for four nights a week, but you will have a positive work situation that can make all the difference, given your professional commitments. This option is one of your two best choices.

Case 5: What Kind of Superintendent Will I Be?

You have been on the fast track, having moved from teacher leader to assistant principal to principal to associate superintendent in record time. Your superintendent is featured in an article by an education editor who seems to have a clear view of how different people shape the superintendency. The education writer did a column in which he identified three superintendent leader styles: (1) the academic visionary who knows how to bring the schools up to date in a fast-changing world; (2) the hands-on leader with special interest in curriculum, instruction, and the nuts and bolts of the classroom; and (3) the politician with slick management patter and an easy way with constituents. The third style, according to the writer, could get along with many different factions and balance their demands so that they feel reasonably, if not totally, satisfied. They all feel that the superintendent is on their side.

What do you see as the strengths of each superintendent leader style and how do you fit into this picture? Please choose from the following options:

1. The academic visionary.

2. The curriculum and instruction leader.

3. The politician.

Case 5: Rationales for the Alternative Responses

1. The academic is up to date on the context in which education and schooling exist. This will be a real plus with long-range planning, for this kind of superintendent will have

not only more encompassing global perspective but also an understanding of the roles that particular organizations can play in relation to the school system. A superintendent with these strengths will be respected for being bright and current. This kind of superintendent will also be highly respected by university scholars and other academics.

2. The superintendent who knows and values curriculum, instruction, and the nuts and bolts of the classroom will have an affinity connection with teachers who place high value on such matters. Many parents will also see this kind of leader as an instructional advocate for their children. After all, schools should have as their primary goal the teaching and learning of children. A superintendent with this expertise will be up to date on the most recent trends in curriculum and instruction and will be able to help teachers and others decide which trends are worth implementing in this school system.

3. The superintendent as politician will be seen as a savvy representative of the political interests of assistant principals, principals, and central office leaders. This superintendent will have his or her feet on the ground and not be led astray by the idealism and romanticism of some teachers and parents. A main advantage of the superintendent as politician is that various factions in the system, factions that can very disruptive and contentious, will be mediated by a real professional who knows how to use power to the ultimate advantage of all concerned. This is probably the best choice given the highly political environment in which schools and schooling now take place.

References

Adams, J. G. (1983). *Without precedent.* New York: Horton.

Anders, G. (2005, February 10). H-P's board ousts Fiorina as CEO: How traits that helped executive climb ladder came to be fatal flaws. *The Wall Street Journal,* pp. A1, A8.

Austin, G., & Brubaker, D. (1988, October). Making the right calls. *PACE, the Magazine of Piedmont Airlines,* 102–106.

Barth, R. S. (2003). *Lessons learned: Shaping relationships and the culture of the workplace.* Thousand Oaks, CA: Corwin Press.

Brubaker, D. (1995, November). How the principalship has changed: Lessons from principals' life stories. *NASSP Bulletin,* 88–95.

Brubaker, D. (2004). *Creative curriculum leadership: Inspiring and empowering your school community.* Thousand Oaks, CA: Corwin Press.

Brubaker, D. (2005). *The charismatic leader: The presentation of self and the creation of educational settings.* Thousand Oaks, CA: Corwin Press.

Brubaker, D., & Coble, L. (1995, October). The derailed superintendent. *The Executive Educator,* 34–36.

Brubaker, D., & Coble, L. (2005). *The hidden leader: Leadership lessons on the potential within.* Thousand Oaks, CA: Corwin Press.

Brubaker, D., & Shelton, M. (1995, February). The disposable superintendent. *The Executive Educator,* 16–19.

Brubaker, D., Simon, L., & Tysinger, N. (1993, May). Principals' leadership styles: The power of the "halo effect." *NASSP Bulletin,* 30–36.

Burgess, S. (1995, May 2). *Constructive forethought and the school administrator.* Speech to the University of North Carolina Alumni Association.

Center for Creative Leadership. (1995). *Benchmark developmental reference points: A developmental learning guide.* Greensboro, NC: Author.

Collins, D. (2000). *Achieving your vision of professional development: How to assess your needs and get what you want.* Greensboro, NC: SERVE.

Conroy, P. (2002). *My losing season.* Garden City, NJ: Doubleday.

Cranston, N. (2000). Teachers as leaders: A critical agenda for the new millennium. *Asia-Pacific Journal of Teacher Education, 28,* 123–132.

163

Darling-Hammond, L. (1997). *The right to learn: A blueprint for creating schools that work.* San Francisco: Jossey-Bass.

Dixon, N. (1995). *A practical model for organizational learning.* Greensboro, NC: Center for Creative Leadership.

Engle, S., & Ochoa, A. (1988). *Education for democratic citizenship.* New York: Teachers College Press.

Fullan, M. (2003). *The moral imperative of school leadership.* Thousand Oaks, CA: Corwin Press.

Gerth, H., & Mills, C. W. (1964). *From Max Weber: Essays in sociology.* New York: Oxford University Press.

Glass, T. (1992). *The study of the American school superintendency: America's education leaders in a time of reform.* Alexandria, VA: Association of School Administrators.

Glickman, C. D. (1990, September). Pushing school reform to a new edge. *Phi Delta Kappan, 68–75.*

Goffman, E. (1959). *The presentation of self in everyday life.* New York: Doubleday.

Goleman, D. (2000). *Working with emotional intelligence.* New York: Bantam.

Greene, L., & Bentley, E. (1987, November). *Upward mobility determinants for the elementary principalship.* Paper presented at the annual meeting of the Southern Regional Council on Educational Administration, Gatlinburg, TN.

Henderson, D. (2005, January 20). [Interview by the authors].

Hood, S. (1996). *Ohio superintendent benchmark data and the derailment issue: An essay.* Greensboro, NC: University of North Carolina Humanistic Education Project.

Hoyle, J. (1988). *The 21st century superintendent: A great motivator. Paul B. Salmon memorial lecture.* Paper presented at the annual meeting of the American Association of School Administrators (AASA). (ERIC Document Reproduction Service No. ED295290)

Hoyle, J, Bjork, L., & Collier, V. (2005). *The superintendent as CEO: Standards-based performance.* Thousand Oaks, CA: Corwin Press.

Huberman, M. (1989, Fall). The professional life cycle of teachers. *Teachers College Record, 31–57.*

Kleinfield, S. (1989). *The hotel.* New York: Simon & Schuster.

Kronholz, J. (2005, January 13). Bush unveils outline of $1.5 billion plan to help high schools. *The Wall Street Journal*, p. D5.

Lane, S. E. (2003). *The impact of a controversial board decision to suspend a school superintendent on the culture and the professional and personal lives of a central office staff in a fast growing school system in the southeastern United States* (2nd ed.). Greensboro, NC: University of North Carolina Humanistic Education Project.

Levinson, D. (1985). *The seasons of a man's life.* New York: Knopf.

Linver, S. (1978). *Speakeasy.* New York: Summit.

Lombardo, M., & Eichinger, R. (1995). *Preventing derailment: What to do before it's too late.* Greensboro, NC: Center for Creative Leadership.

Lortie, D. (1995, Winter). Teaching educational administration: Reflections on our craft [The Mitstifer Lecture, sponsored by the Pennsylvania State University and the University Council for Educational Administration]. *UCEA Review,* 5–9, 12.

Mailer, N. (2005, January 23). One idea. *Parade,* 4–6.

May, R. (1975). *The courage to be.* New York: Bantam.

McCall, M., Jr., & Lombardo, M. (1983). *Off the track: Why and how successful executives get derailed* (Technical Report No. 21). Greensboro, NC: Center for Creative Leadership.

McCall, M., Jr., Lombardo, M., & Morrison, A. (1988). *The lessons of experience.* Lexington, MA: Lexington Books.

Moe, T. M. (2005, January 13). No teacher left behind. *The Wall Street Journal,* p. A12.

Moser, D. (2005). *The search for a principal's inner curriculum* (2nd ed.). Greensboro, NC: University of North Carolina Humanistic Education Project.

Nolan, F. (2005). *Looking back at the assistant principalship* (2nd ed.). Greensboro, NC: University of North Carolina Humanistic Education Project.

O'Callaghan, W. (1996, February 1). [An opinion survey of Ohio school superintendents presented to John M. Goff, Superintendent of Public Instruction, Ohio Department of Education].

Peck, M. S. (1978). *The road less traveled.* New York: Simon & Schuster.

Peck, M. S. (1993). *A world waiting to be born: Civility rediscovered.* New York: Bantam.

Rabkin, N., & Redmond, R. (2005, January 15). The art of school success. *Greensboro News & Record,* p. A9.

Renchler, R. (1992). *Urban superintendents' turnover: The need for stability.* Washington, DC: Office of Educational Research and Improvement. (ERIC Document Reproduction Service No. ED346546)

Sarason, S. (1972). *The creation of settings and the future societies.* San Francisco: Jossey-Bass.

Sarason, S. (1995). *Parental involvement and the political principle: Why the existing governance structure of schools should be abolished.* San Francisco: Jossey-Bass.

Sarason, S. (1996). *Barometers of change: Individual, educational and social transformation.* San Francisco: Jossey-Bass.

Schieffer, B. (2003). *This just in: What I couldn't tell you on TV.* New York: Putnam.

Schlesinger, A. M., Jr. (2000). *A life in the twentieth century: Innocent beginnings.* Boston: Houghton Mifflin.

Senge, P. (1990). *The fifth discipline: The art and practice of the learning organization.* New York: Doubleday.

Shulman, L. (1995, March 16). *The case for national curriculum standards.* Lecture at the University of North Carolina at Greensboro's School of Education.

Simmons, T. (1995, November 2). Elite teachers facing burnout: Large percentage of teaching fellows seek new careers. *Raleigh News and Observer,* 1.

Smith, H. (1988). *The power game.* New York: Random House.

Stake, R. (1995). *The art of case study research.* Thousand Oaks, CA: Sage.

Steinem, G. (1992). *Revolution from within: A book of self-esteem.* Boston: Little, Brown.

Tell, C. (2001, February). Appreciating good teaching. *Educational Leadership, 58,* 6–11.

Thomas, R. M. (2005). *High-stakes testing: Coping with collateral damage.* Mahwah, NJ: Lawrence Erlbaum.

Welsh, P. (1987). *Tales out of school.* New York: Penguin.

Index

**CORWIN
PRESS**

The Corwin Press logo—a raven striding across an open book—represents the union of courage and learning. Corwin Press is committed to improving education for all learners by publishing books and other professional development resources for those serving the field of PreK–12 education. By providing practical, hands-on materials, Corwin Press continues to carry out the promise of its motto: **"Helping Educators Do Their Work Better."**